BATH
AT WAR 1939–45

This book is dedicated to our parents
Gordon [1929-2017] and Gillian Brenda [1929-2015]
who lived their entire lives in Bath

The authors' parents.

YOUR TOWNS & CITIES IN WORLD WAR TWO

BATH

AT WAR 1939–45

NIGEL AND DAVID LASSMAN

Pen & Sword
MILITARY

AN IMPRINT OF PEN & SWORD BOOKS LTD.
YORKSHIRE – PHILADELPHIA

First published in Great Britain in 2018 by
Pen & Sword Military
An imprint of
Pen & Sword Books Ltd
Yorkshire – Philadelphia

ISBN 978 1 52670 628 7

A CIP catalogue record for this book is
available from the British Library.

Printed and bound in England
By CPI Group (UK) Ltd, Croydon, CR0 4YY
Typeset by Aura Technology and Software Services, India

Pen & Sword Books Limited incorporates the imprints of Atlas, Archaeology,
Aviation, Discovery, Family History, Fiction, History, Maritime, Military, Military
Classics, Politics, Select, Transport, True Crime, Air World, Frontline Publishing,
Leo Cooper, Remember When, Seaforth Publishing, The Praetorian Press,
Wharncliffe Local History, Wharncliffe Transport, Wharncliffe True Crime and
White Owl.

For a complete list of Pen & Sword titles please contact

PEN & SWORD BOOKS LIMITED
47 Church Street, Barnsley, South Yorkshire, S70 2AS, England
E-mail: enquiries@pen-and-sword.co.uk
Website: www.pen-and-sword.co.uk

Or
PEN AND SWORD BOOKS
1950 Lawrence Rd, Havertown, PA 19083, USA
E-mail: Uspen-and-sword@casematepublishers.com
Website: www.penandswordbooks.com

Contents

Introduction

When travelling abroad, most people will, at some time or another, be asked where they come from. On relaying this information there will normally be one of two reactions on the face of the person asking the question: either a blank stare or a smile of recognition. Being able to say 'Bath' as your home town brings with it not only the knowledge that you live in one of the most beautiful and historically important cities in the world, but also that you will encounter, most times, the latter reaction.

The city of Bath, along with London and Stratford-upon-Avon, is one of the three places in England everyone knows; with anywhere else in this island being a matter of chance. An apocryphal story this might be, but worth the telling none the less: A resident of Bristol going to foreign climes travels through various countries. He is asked by the inhabitants where he comes from and, again and again, it is blank stares he receives. Even when he says that the place he hails from was voted by *The Sunday Times* in 2017 the best place to live in the whole of Britain, he receives the same reaction. It is only when it is clarified by the person saying 'Bristol, near Bath' that he receives the reaction normally accorded to actual residents of this 'near' city.

To most people Bath represents one of two historic periods – the Roman or the Georgian; both having left behind world famous and iconic monuments which are the main reasons almost a million tourists visit the city every year. When we were growing up in the 1960s, Bath was still known as the Roman City. The Roman Baths were seemingly the centre of the city's universe and visits to, or school projects about them were a regular occurrence. It is only through the promotion in more recent years of the city's connection with Jane Austen that its Georgian period has been catapulted into the same league as the Roman. For the authors of this book however, as true Bathonians – having been born and educated here – the city also represents another historic period: that of the Second World War onwards. Our learning was not done in any classroom, but rather at home, through stories, memories and the reminiscences of our parents, both of whom lived through the time this book covers. For us, the entire war – its announcement, the 'Phoney War', Dunkirk, the Battle of Britain, the Bath Blitz, the Leroy Henry case, VE Day, VJ Day, etc – can only be experienced second-hand.

The War Memorial at Haycombe Cemetery.

For our mother and father, growing up in wartime in Weston village and Lower Swainswick (respectively), these events formed the fabric of their early lives. We also had other relatives who served, and we have woven their stories into this account wherever we can. It is to our eternal regret that our parents are no longer alive to see this book in print, or our dedication of it to them; but we had been commissioned to write it *before* our father died and so the final period of his life allowed an opportunity to recall his stories once more and to clarify any details we were uncertain about. We only hope that we have done them proud with this book and that on reading it they would have said, 'Yes, that is how it was.'

One aspect of the war did have a major impact on the lives of both authors. On leaving school the authors went to work for the Admiralty, as so many other school leavers also did; it was still located in the city several decades after being evacuated there in September 1939. Although still resident at the time in the Empire Hotel, the main sites the Admiralty occupied within the city remained Foxhill, Warminster Road and Ensleigh. One of the authors spent time at the first, before transferring to the second, while the other author worked for three years at the latter. All three sites have now sadly gone though, and at the time of writing are in the process of being replaced by residential housing.

The authors' grandfather (Ernest Lassman) and uncle (Ronald Lassman); both served in the RAF during the war.

There are other books on this period of the city's history available, indeed some with similar titles, most notably those by David and Jonathan Falconer. Although worthwhile reads, we feel our book has something additional to offer. Whereas their first book, *Bath at War*, relied heavily – on their own admission – on the newspaper archives of the *Bath and Wilts Chronicle and Herald*, with the book's structure sectioning the various aspects of the city's wartime experience into separate chapters, their second, *Bath at War: The Home Front*, relied almost exclusively on personal anecdotes and reminiscences to recount the same story.

What we have done with this book is to give a linear structure to the narrative – starting in September 1939 with the declaration of war and ending not long after VJ Day and the cessation of hostilities – while putting the events happening on the home front within the larger context of the various theatres of war. Through approaching the story like this, it is hoped the reader who was not there can experience the various ups and downs, the victories and defeats, and other elements that occurred in Bath during this time in a way – although thoroughly condensed and second-hand – which gives at least some idea of what it must have been like to live through Bath at war in 1939-45.

Nigel & David Lassman
April 2018

Left: The Empire Hotel was one of the buildings requisitioned by the Admiralty when they moved down from London.

Below: One of the mass graves of Bath Blitz victims.

CHAPTER 1

Declaration (September 1939)

As history records it, Britain declared war on Germany at 11 o'clock on Sunday the 3rd of September 1939, and so for the people of Bath, along with the rest of the country, that is when the Second World War officially began.

The declaration and the war had not come out of the blue. Like the First World War, which had ended two decades earlier and involved men and women from the city, events had been pointing towards conflict during the preceding few years. This time around, demands since the mid-1930s by Germany and its leader, Adolf Hitler, had tested the resolve of the British government and although Prime Minister Neville Chamberlain had sought appeasement throughout this period, it was not through personal weakness, as is often believed, but because he knew the country was weak and not yet militarily resourced for war. So, as during the period leading to the previous conflict, the government used these pre-war years to instigate a programme of rearmament and adequately prepare its defences.

Unlike the First World War, these preparations now had to take into consideration the civilian population. The devastating effects of Zeppelin attacks on several English coastal towns near the end of that former war cannot be overstated and this was reinforced by more recent images from the Spanish Civil War, which showed just how much devastation and destruction could be inflicted on cities from the air.

With this potential threat in the forefront of the authorities' minds, Bath City Council had been tasked with the creation of the ARP (Air Raid Precautions). This organisation, initially based at 2 Broad Street, oversaw all aspects of civil defence. This included the distribution of 70,000 gas masks throughout the city and, during the summer of 1939, taking part in a 'feigned state of emergency' that consisted of an imaginary air raid, with numerous counties taking part, including Somerset, Wiltshire, Gloucestershire and Dorset. With all preparations thus completed, the council could state authoritatively, once war finally arrived, that 'In the absence of an actual attack to test the effectiveness of the machinery, everything possible has been done to ensure the safety of our population in an emergency'.

The declaration of war meant reservists across the city received their mobilisation orders. These were men who were presently serving in the Territorial

Army, or else had previously been in the armed forces but had left or retired, with the stipulation they could be recalled in the event of war. For Bath's population it must have felt like history was repeating itself. Most no doubt remembered only too vividly waving off their husbands, sons, boyfriends, fiancés, fathers, brothers, uncles, nephews, friends and work colleagues back in 1914 – many of whom were never to return – and now, a quarter of a century later, they were about to do the same again. This time though, a completely different atmosphere prevailed in the city. As one local resident would record, 'This is a most peculiar war and as different from the 1914 affair as one could possibly imagine. There is no exuberant patriotism, no flag waving or cheering crowds, yet every man woman & child is calm and determined.'

Whereas numerous Bath men had volunteered at the outbreak of the First World War – responding to Lord Kitchener's famous patriotic call to arms – the government was (rightly) taking no chances on being able to elicit such patriotic fever again, and two days after Poland was invaded parliament passed the National Service (Armed Forces) Act. This meant that Bath men between the ages of 18 and 41, unless already in the forces or a reserved occupation, were eligible to be called up.

So, once again, Bath men (and women) set off for theatres of war that would encompass the globe and during the first weeks of September 1939, trains taking them across the country to join regiments, ships or squadrons, headed out from the city's two main railway stations. Some left from the old 'Midland' station (later known as Green Park) serviced by the London, Midland & Scotland (LMS) and the Somerset & Dorset (S&D) railway companies; their trains headed north or south. Others left from Bath Spa, at the bottom of Manvers Street; their trains headed east and west and were owned by the Great Western Railway (GWR).

Along with conscription from the outset of war, there would be other differences between this conflict and the previous one. Perhaps the greatest of these, as time would show, was that the death and destruction witnessed on the battlefields by men and women from the city during the First World War – and during this one too – would also be experienced by those on the home front: the true horrors of war delivered, quite literally in numerous cases, right to people's front doors. Although the coastal towns attacked by Germany during the First World War had experienced the terrifying ordeal of aerial bombardment, many inland ones, along with major cities including Bath, would now be recipients.

Although the war officially began on the third day of September, Hitler's invasion of Poland two days earlier had triggered several contingency plans to be put into action. One of these was Operation Pied Piper: the evacuation of children, and others, from cities deemed vulnerable to German aerial attack, such as

Civil Defence leaflet explaining the evacuation.

London, to places of perceived safety. The plan had been conceived in May 1938 by the Home Secretary Sir John Anderson, who would also give his name to the corrugated-steel air-raid shelter. It would become the largest mass movement of people in British history, an exodus dwarfing even the biblical one, according to one newspaper. Under the scheme, the country was divided into three areas: Evacuation, Neutral and Reception. Despite the preparations undertaken by its council, Bath and the surrounding areas were not considered to be at risk and so had been placed in the latter category. Through the summer of 1939, therefore, families had been sought to become hosts to the evacuees in the event of war.

Operation Pied Piper produced some of the most iconic images of the conflict – those of schoolchildren, in groups or alone, standing on platforms with suitcases in their hands or by their sides. As accurate and vivid a portrayal of the evacuation as these images were, it is a misconception to think that it was only the young who were moved. Not only did the government intend to evacuate schoolchildren but also their teachers – in many cases, entire schools were transferred to safety – along with pre-school children, accompanied by their mothers or responsible adults, expectant mothers and adults who were blind or crippled, so far as their removal was feasible.

As soon as the British government received news that Germany had crossed the Polish border, the evacuation plan became operational, and on that Friday, 1 September 1939, and over the following weekend, trains poured out of London and other cites to more rural destinations in the countryside. By the time war was officially declared two days later, more than one and a half million people had become evacuees, with nearly 7,000 having arrived at Bath. The Pavilion was requisitioned for use as an administrative centre and many schools, including those in South Twerton, Kingsmead, Bathwick and Widcombe, were temporarily converted into distribution centres.

Five trains a day were scheduled to arrive at Bath Spa Station throughout the evacuation period, each containing approximately 800 children, with the first expected around noon. When the first train arrived on that Friday, a little later than expected, hundreds of Bath people were there to greet them, including huge numbers of the city's own schoolchildren, along with the mayor – Captain Adrian Hopkins – and his wife. It came from Ealing, in London, carrying the pupils of two schools from the Shepherd's Bush area and as the *Bath Chronicle* would later report, 'As the coaches drew up at the platform, there were cheers from the carriages and a forest of hands waving a salutation to Bath.' As hundreds of children and their teachers alighted from the carriages, the station platform quickly filled up with not only bodies, but also respirators, haversacks, kit-bags, cases and teaching equipment; cheering from the waiting locals mingled with the sound of megaphones and whistles, as the task of dispersing the children began.

Out of the 800 arrivals, as would be standard practice throughout the evacuation period, 280 were due to be billeted in the city, with the rest taken to more rural areas, such as Keynsham, Clutton and Radstock. Those remaining in Bath were ushered outside to be taken to the appropriate distribution centre. For those whose schools were nearby, such as Widcombe, a short walk entailed, but for others, whose destinations were further away, fleets of coaches and private cars were waiting. Once at the distribution centres, the children were given a hot meal and assigned to their host families. They were then taken away to what would be their new homes for the foreseeable future.

All the children had been given emergency rations for the first 48 hours, which some had already eaten on the train, consisting of one can of meat, two cans of milk (one sweetened and one unsweetened), one pound of biscuits and a quarter pound of chocolate. For adults, such as a mother and child, the allowance was the same, except they received two cans of meat. Children were also given a stamped postcard on their arrival, to send back home, so as to let their parents know where they had ended up, as the majority of evacuees were not told of their destination until they arrived in the city.

Host families in Bath, as elsewhere, received *10s 6d* a week for taking in an unaccompanied child, or *8s 6d* a week for each child where more than one child was taken. Where there was a parent or responsible adult with the child, the hosts received *6s* a week for each adult and *3s* a week for each child. Householders providing lodgings for teachers or helpers would receive *5s* a week.

Altogether during the evacuation period 6,717 evacuees came through the receiving area of Bath and were distributed as follows: Bath 2,296; Bathavon 1,439; Clutton 1,928; Keynsham 770; Radstock 284. Everything went according to plan it seemed, as the *Bath Chronicle* was able to report that 'The reception was carried out without mishap and all the evacuees for Bath were billeted on the day of their arrival.'

Not only did the government have to look after vulnerable civilian groups, they also had to take care of their own personnel. Some years earlier they had looked for safe areas in the country to which certain Admiralty departments could be relocated, if necessary. The criteria required of such places included being situated on a main railway line located two to three hours travel time from London and containing numerous buildings suitable for requisitioning as offices and accommodation. Bath, perhaps unsurprisingly, came to the authorities' attention quite early on in their search, fulfilling all criteria more than adequately. The reason all these facilities were in place was due to the city being a major tourist destination. Ironically, the very qualities which made Bath so attractive to the government as a 'safe haven', also earned it a place in the German 'Baedeker' Tourist Guide; a fact that would have dire consequences for the city later in the war.

And so, with the advent of war, the British government moved several of its departments to Bath. Those to be relocated from London were mostly within the Admiralty and specifically those of Ship Design and Naval Stores. It was arranged that these departments would take over various hotels and other buildings in the city, including the old Tram Shed at the bottom of Walcot Street, the trams having ceased running from there earlier that year. Each hotel was designated with a number and prefixed by the letters 'AA', which stood for Bath. Near the end of September 1939, almost 4,000 Admiralty staff, and in many cases also their families, arrived in the city. This included the Bannisters, whose son Roger would later become the first man to break the four-minute mile barrier in athletics.

For the most part, the evacuees – Admiralty personnel and civilians – integrated themselves amicably with the residents of the city, who continued their daily lives under the auspices of war. That is not to say issues did not arise – the scarcity of accommodation probably being one of the biggest. Although many had left the city for the war, their families were still housed in the accommodation they had left. Along with the newly arrived evacuees – both civilians and Admiralty – there were several other large groups who had become temporary residents. These included large numbers of Irish workers, brought over to help convert underground facilities on the outskirts of the city, refugees disposed from their homelands by Hitler's pre-war occupations (and more were to follow), and children brought out from Germany on what became known as the *Kindertransport* scheme.

Despite several letters and complaints to the local newspapers, most Bath citizens accepted this overcrowding, along with everything else, as part of the

The Admiralty arrive at the Empire Hotel.

wartime effort. As one *Bath Chronicle* reporter, writing from the newspaper's offices at 33 Westgate Street, noted, 'The city retains its dignity, but an air of busy efficiency has been given to its bustling streets that have changed its character from a spa to a city conscious of its duties and obligations to the visitors.' With the influx of so many outsiders, mainly Londoners, the reporter observed the place had acquired a sense of the capital's busy streets, along with its cosmopolitan character.

Bath was no stranger to visitors from London or indeed from elsewhere around the world and had flourished through earlier centuries because of them. Having been given the royal seal of approval through two visits by Queen Anne at the beginning of the eighteenth century, the previously small medieval town had quickly become, during the subsequent Georgian period, the most fashionable destination outside London for society's upper echelon. The middle classes soon followed, leading to a population explosion in the city not experienced again until the start of this Second World War and the influx of evacuees. The status royally bestowed on eighteenth-century Bath also gave rise to a building programme whose spectacular architecture became the envy of the world. One of the main proponents of this, along with father and son architects, John Wood the Elder and Younger, was Ralph Allen, whose quarries at Combe Down would provide the stone that would give the city's buildings their distinctive honey-coloured look. Allen subsequently used Bath stone to build the Prior Park on one of the hills overlooking the city so as 'to see all Bath and for all Bath to see'. This Palladian mansion became both his home and an example to the attributes of the material he mined. Prior Park was badly damaged during the blitz, but was repaired and is today an educational centre, with the surrounding parkland owned by the National Trust.

A tradition from that Georgian era, which had survived to the beginning of the war, was the 'Bath chair'. These were specially insulated carriages for conveying patients from their hotels to the spa treatment centres – for which, along with its architecture, the city was world famous – and back again, without significantly lowering body temperature or having to be seen in public. Operated by 'chairmen', they were originally physically carried, but later pulled, through the streets (or else through the underground tunnels that connected certain hotels with the spa centres) and were licensed in the same way as modern-day taxis. The first chairs appeared in 1780 and by Victorian times 162 were licensed with the local authorities. By the 1930s this dwindled to between 50 and 60. The arrival of the Admiralty and their requisitioning of many hotels meant the end of this institution, as the elderly who normally used the chairs were displaced and the civil servants who took over had no use for them.

rior Park College, Bath.

Above: Prior Park

Below: Ralph Allen's sprawling mansion was badly damaged during the Bath Blitz.

Another item that vanished from the streets of Bath was the bulbs housed in street lamps. These were taken out, wrapped up and put into storage for the duration of the war (sadly, when eventually unwrapped, most would be unusable). This was part of the almost draconian regulations that enforced the blackout – the measures taken to ensure that enemy planes would not be guided to the city.

When a national newspaper ran a poll a couple of months into the war, asking its readers what they hated most about the war, the 'blackout' topped most people's lists. All premises – residential or business – had to have proper coverings, making sure not a chink of light emanated from within between the times of half an hour after sunset until half an hour before sunrise. ARP wardens patrolled to ensure these regulations were adhered to and those caught breaking them were severely dealt with.

There was no part of daily city life unaffected by the blackout. Church services, in many cases, were rearranged or suspended indefinitely, while parking restrictions in the centre led to the situation where vehicles were allowed to park on one side of the street on odd dates and the other side on even dates.

There were positive aspects to the blackout: the night sky could be seen more clearly without light pollution and, as cars became more difficult to use, bicycles and horse-drawn traffic multiplied, giving many older people a sense

The pre-war painting of white rings around tree trunks in preparation for the black-out

of a throwback to an earlier age. However, despite tree trunks and pavement kerbs being painted with white markings, accidents due to the blackout became a daily part of city life. Countless pedestrians suffered minor bumps and scrapes sustained from walking into trees in the dark or tripping off kerbs, and the *Bath Chronicle* was full of reports of more serious and often fatal incidents.

In September 1939, the number of people killed nationwide in road accidents doubled, and between October and December, 4,133 people lost their lives, compared to 2,497 in the same period the previous year. The figure for December 1939 alone was 1,155. Bath was not immune, with several fatalities, including one at Weston village, where our mother lived. These statistics, as bad as they were, did not give the full picture, as they excluded people who fell through roofs while on fire duty, from trains at railway stations, or those who accidentally fell into canals or rivers.

One incident, involving the Kennet and Avon canal, befell a Mr Gledhill. The unfortunate man was near one of the Widcombe locks, in the south-east of the city, during the blackout, when he inadvertently fell in. His cries for help were thankfully heard by a nearby garage proprietor, Mr Wood, who drove one of the cars from the garage to the canal bank. According the report in the newspaper report, he 'switched on the head lights to shine on the dark water and plunged in.' Messrs Gledhill and Wood survived, with the latter receiving an award from the Royal Humane Society for his bravery.

Not everyone who had the misfortune to fall into the canal was so lucky. In May 1940, 5-year-old Terence Newman was walking home from his school at Widcombe when, for some unknown reason, he fell into one of the locks near to where he lived. A school friend sounded the alarm and in no time at all people were at the scene, including Terence's own mother. John Stacy, an employee from nearby Widcombe Garage dived in and tried to help pull the youngster to safety. However, the boy began to struggle and, in danger of losing his own life as well, the garage worker had to admit defeat and let go. 'I was nearly done when they dragged me out,' Stacy later told a reporter. 'He clung round my neck and was pulling me under. I had to let him go.' A Lance Corporal Jones and several police officers tried to locate the boy, and when Terence's body was finally found an hour later and pulled from the water, he was dead.

Although the number of motor accidents had risen, the actual number of cars on the road had fallen dramatically and the main mode of transport for people, other than pedal or horse power, was buses and trains (the city's tram system having by now been scrapped – literally, as its lines would soon be torn up). Austerity buses, as they were known, became a familiar sight, each being able to carry twice the number of people normally accommodated in a single decker, and overall the bus companies increased their services through the day (although limited them more at night). Rail travel also saw a dramatic increase during the war; within a few years, it would be as much as 70 per cent up on pre-war levels. With this increase in demand though, trains were more oft to break down and crowding became almost unbearable during peak times, such as Christmas and Easter breaks, when families would travel to visit evacuated loved ones, or when returning to their own from the front.

There is at least one aspect from the blackout, other than overcrowded trains, which has survived until the present day. With thousands of civil servants suddenly having to live and work in a strange community, and in the surreal conditions of the darkened city nights, there was the potential for trouble or mishap. The naval authorities, having noticed the locals played a game called skittles, the object of which was to throw three balls along a wooden alley to knock down as many as possible of the nine pins (or skittles) at the end of it, decided to instigate their own league. Not only would this give their personnel something to do in the evenings, they surmised, but it would hopefully foster team spirit. Most sections within the Admiralty departments were able to find enough players to form a team (eight was the usual number) and in a short space of time the Admiralty Skittles League was up and running. So successful was it that nearly eighty years later the league is still going strong and, somewhat incredibly, several teams retain their wartime designations, including the E-in-C (Engineer-in-Chief), DNC (Director of Naval Construction) and DEE III (Director of Electrical Engineering 3).

Despite the bumps, cuts, grazes and the occasional fatality, life in wartime Bath seemed protected from the realities of the war going on elsewhere. This did not last long though, as the city's first taste of the stark horrors of the conflict came in the middle of September 1939, when HMS *Courageous* was sunk by a German submarine, 300 miles west of Land's End. Nearly 600 men died when the ship went down, including several men from Bath.

HMS *Courageous* had been built during the First World War, the lead ship of the cruiser class named after it. Decommissioned once that war ended, the ship was rebuilt as an aircraft carrier in the 1920s, capable of carrying nearly fifty aircraft. For a while she had been a training vessel, but at the start of this latest war served with the Home Fleet, carrying two Squadrons – 811 and 822 – each equipped with a dozen Fairey Swordfish. HMS *Courageous* left Plymouth on 3 September, escorted by four destroyers, to embark on anti-submarine patrols. Fourteen days later she was attacked by the U-boat. The enemy fired three torpedoes, two of which struck the ship on its port side. It quickly capsized and sank within twenty minutes, taking with it nearly half its crew, including its captain.

The dead included naval and RAF personnel, both represented by men from the city. One of the latter was 31-year-old Edward John Leslie Bath, an aircraftsman second class. He was serving as a flight mechanic aboard the ship and had been in the RAF for seventeen months. He was married to Eileen and they had two young children – a boy aged 4 and a 2-year-old girl. The family lived in Combe Down on the southern outskirts of the city and before joining the armed forces Edward had been a garage and taxi proprietor. He is listed on the Royal Air Force memorial to the missing at Runnymede in Surrey. Also in the RAF, but remembered on the Fleet Air Arm Memorial at Lee-on-Solent was Bernard John Owen. The Petty Officer was 34 years of age and married to Ivy. He was an observer with the Fleet Air Arm when he lost his life.

The loss of HMS Courageous and some of the men on it.

The rest of the fatalities from Bath were all in the Royal Navy. Able Seaman Percy Walter Minns, 44, who lived in Ivy Avenue, located upon one of the south slopes of the city, was called up at the beginning of the war, having been in the RN Reserve; before that he had been a highly respected postman. John Keeling, Stoker First Class, had lost two brothers in the previous war, both killed in action, and the 39-year-old was due to have been discharged back in August, before the threat of war stopped it. He was a widower and left a 15-year-old daughter. Other fatalities were 47-year-old George Eacott, Cyril Morgan, 21, and Victor Lawley, all who, like John Keeling, held the position of stoker first class, and Able Seaman Ronald Pritchard, who was a year older than Morgan. He was the son of Leonard and Gwen Pritchard of Bath. His name appears on the Plymouth Naval Memorial, on Plymouth Hoe, along with all the others above.

The survivors also included men from the city. Patrick Quintin, who lived in Camden Cottages and was recently married, survived in the water for around two hours after *Courageous* sank, eventually being pulled to safety by personnel on one of the accompanying destroyers. A newspaper account reported that on his return to the city he visited the place of his pre-war employment – Stothert and Pitt – to see his old colleagues.

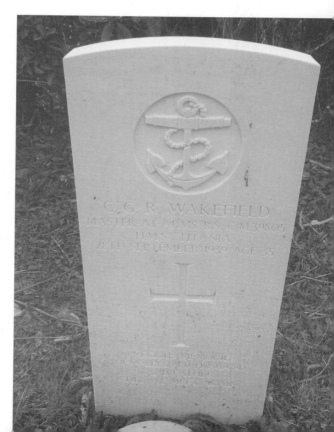

The grave of C.G.R Wakefield, who was killed when his ship Titania *was sunk near the end of September 1939, only a few weeks after the start of the war.*

Eleven days later, another sinking, that of HMS *Titania*, saw the loss of a further local man – Master-at-Arms Charles Gilbert Robert Wakefield. Originally from Oxford, he was 36 years old and left a wife, Mabel, a son and two daughters, all of whom lived at 6, St Saviour's Terrace, in Bath. He is buried in St Michael's cemetery in Lower Weston.

Friday, 29 September 1939, the day after Charles Wakefield was killed, became known as National Registration Day. This was instigated by the government to issue identity cards to eligible citizens and for any future food rationing, which they were intent on introducing. Each household filled out a schedule to be collected by enumerators. The National Registration Act had been passed at the beginning of the month, but, no doubt due to the magnitude of the task of recording the 46 million people who would be affected it, it had taken the rest of September to make the necessary arrangements. Identity cards would be issued the following month and every person in the city who had one was required always to carry it on their person.

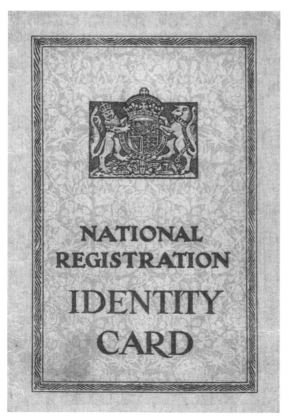

National identity cards had to be carried by everyone.

N.R. 50.

NATIONAL REGISTER.

NATIONAL REGISTRATION DAY IS FRIDAY, 29th SEPTEMBER, 1939.

SEE INSTRUCTIONS IN SCHEDULE AS TO " PERSONS TO BE INCLUDED."

RATIONING.—The return on the schedule herewith will be used not only for National Registration but also for Food Rationing purposes. It is to your interest, therefore, as well as your public duty, to fill up the return carefully, fully and accurately.

Help the Enumerator to collect the schedule promptly by arranging for him to receive it when he calls. Do not make it necessary for him to call a number of times before he can obtain it.

When the Enumerator collects the schedule, he must write and deliver an Identity Card for every person included in the return. Help him to write them properly for you by letting him write at a table.

If the whole household moves before the schedule is collected, take it with you and hand it to the Enumerator calling at your new residence or to the National Registration Office for your new address. The address of this office can be ascertained at a local police station.

Wt 28033—171   12 50

National Registration Day

CHAPTER 2

Anticipation & Evacuation
(October 1939 – May 1940)

The beginning of October 1939 saw an increase in hostilities, although this was not on a battlefield but in the chambers of Bath City Council. The opposing forces were those of the city's councillors and the members of the recently formed Emergency Committee.

The Emergency Committee had come into existence because of the war and its remit was to make the decisions regarding all aspects of the city's civil defence; this included the financial control of the ARP. The three-man committee – the 'Big Three' as they swiftly became known – consisted of the mayor (who at this time was still Captain Hopkins) and two councillors – Major Geoffrey Lock and Major Walter Barrett.

At this third of October meeting the committee was accused of various misdemeanours, including 'extravagance, wasting money and favouritism', the latter accusation connected to the employment of full-time ARP staff. Although this 'attack' on the Big Three was cited by the local newspaper as being of a 'vigour rarely heard in the council', they were able to state that the mayor had defended the accusations against the Emergency Committee with just as much energy. Hopkins would use his final speech in the position, the following month, to criticise what he called the 'ARP baiters'.

The committee members had been accused of weilding their power 'dictatorially' and at one stage during the heated meeting, Alderman Hunt had declared, 'We are fighting a war to get rid of one dictator but we have put three in his place. We have got Mussolini, Hitler and Stalin.' Alderman Aubrey Bateman was then heard to ask, to resultant laughter in the chamber, 'Which is which?' The irony of this question might not have been lost on him the following year when he himself became mayor (succeeding James Carpenter LLD who, in his turn, had succeeded Hopkins) and therefore one of the 'Big Three'.

The city's first Christmas of the war proceeded as normally as could be expected, although obviously within the tight regulations of the blackout and the absence of so many loved ones. There were certain surreal aspects to the festive period, as shops in the city were only allowed to light their window displays early in the morning, while people were on their way to work. Night displays were strictly forbidden due to the blackout.

The Post Office, anticipating a huge surge in demand for their services across the festive period, and feeling the pressure of employee shortages, advertised for both staff and the early posting of parcels, letters and cards.

A Christmas visit by royalty was bestowed upon Bath in the middle of December, but unlike Queen Anne, at the beginning of the eighteenth century, who had arrived to take the famous waters, Queen Mary and members of the royal household were visiting the city for another of its famous attractions: shopping. The trip included well-known shops such as Jollys in Milsom Street, Colmers in Union Street and Woolworths located in Stall Street. In the latter, Queen Mary was escorted around the store by its manager Mr T. Kirkpatrick, purchasing well over fifty items. She was no stranger to the area, having a residence not far away at Badminton and visiting on several occasions previously, including recently near the end of October to two city hospitals: the RUH (Royal United Hospital) and the Forbes-Fraser.

Whether any gloves or other warm attire had been purchased by Queen Mary on her Christmas shopping trip is not recorded, but they were certainly needed in the New Year, as the winter would be the coldest for forty-five years. The bad weather began during the first week of January 1940 and in a fortnight was so cold the River Thames froze for the first time since 1888. Milk froze solid on doorsteps and coal supplies ran out.

The weather only added to the miserable start of the year. On New Year's Day, more men from Bath found themselves being called up, this time between the ages of 19 and 27. They were among the two million men nationwide who received their papers at this time. And the day after the bad weather began, food rationing was introduced. There had been attempts to bring it in earlier – it was originally going to be introduced in November 1939 and then December, but on both occasions had been postponed, as the government was concerned about the public's reaction. On 8 January 1940, however, rationing became a way of life for the city's population and incredibly would not be completely lifted for more than fourteen years, eight years after the war ended.

The first items to be rationed were butter, sugar, bacon and ham, followed a couple of months later by other meats and then even later by cheese and additional foodstuffs. Rationing of meat and cheese would be the cause of the most complaints in the city. Allowances for various items would fluctuate throughout the war, and the *Bath Chronicle* would print recipes or advice on how people could make the most of their allowances.

As the first months of 1940 wore on, there was still no major activity on land or in the air and several names were coined for this time of inaction. The 'Bore' (no doubt paraphrasing the Boer War, which had taken place at the beginning of the century) and the 'Twilight' war were two of them, but most people would come to know this period as the 'Phoney War'.

Most people knew that it would not be until spring, and more clement weather, that Hitler would make any move on land.

There were, of course, still hostile confrontations and resultant casualties that involved men from the city, but mostly these took place at sea. Although Bath is an inland city, miles from the nearest coast, its connection with the maritime world was strong even before the arrival of the Admiralty a few months earlier and had been for several centuries.

An earlier, darker side of this seafaring link saw it as benefactor of, and contributor to, the transatlantic slave trade and one third of the triangle also comprising Bristol and London. Many of the city's landmarks and buildings, such as Beckford's Tower and Great Pulteney Street, for example, along with many of the latter's wealthy inhabitants and owners, owed their existence and prosperity to this barbaric trade.

A more honourable association was with Lord Horatio Nelson, who spent many periods of time in the city, of which he had been given the freedom, when not securing great naval victories.

By the beginning of 1940, the city had lost several more of its naval sons. HMS *Courageous* and HMS *Titania* had been sunk in the first few weeks of the war and on 23 November 1939 the *Rawalpindi* (an armed merchant cruiser) was sunk by the German warships *Scharnhorst* and *Gneisenau*. Captain E.C. Kennedy and 270 of the crew were killed, including 40-year-old Douglas S. Farrant of Bath. The Seaman Gunner had been a platelayer on the Great Western Railway before the war and was a member of the Bath branch of the White Ensign Association. As a member of the Royal Naval Reserve, he served in the Navy throughout the First World War and had taken part in the Battle of Jutland aboard HMS *New Zealand*. By a strange coincidence, the captain of the *Rawalpindi* when she was sunk, E.C. Kennedy, had been the man in charge of HMS *New Zealand* back in 1916. Farrant left a widow, a boy and two little girls, aged 10, 6 and 4. They lived at 113 High Street, Upper Weston, and had done so for the previous four and a half years, having moved there from Caledonian Road in Twerton.

Although the sinking of *Courageous* in September was a particularly bitter blow to the city, with so many Bath men losing their lives, there had been survivors; as was the case in the sinking of the HMS *Royal Oak* the following month. Despite the loss of more than 800 crew of the 29,500-ton battleship, several local men survived. For the parents of one marine, the news was initially bleak. Mr and Mrs Herbert Baber of Kelston Mills received two messages to the effect that their son had gone down with the ship. A few days later, however, a message was received from their offspring saying that he was very much alive.

Another Royal Marine survivor was 33-year-old father of three, Reginald Turner, of 31 Thomas Street, Bath. A graphic description of his experience appeared in the *Bath Chronicle* towards the end of October:

Royal Marine Reginald Turner who survived the sinking of HMS Royal Oak.

> I was asleep in my hammock and was awakened by a dull explosion about 1.05am on Oct. 14th. The next and heavier explosion came about 1.15 and then the ship began to tilt over badly. There was no panic at all, but we had to be quick and jump over the side of the vessel which was keeling over badly by then. Some accounts of the sinking said that it was fairly light, but actually it was pitch dark at the time with not much of a tide. With men all around me in the water, I managed to hold on to the side and then swim away; five minutes later the Royal Oak was sunk in a terrific flurry of water. I swam about for a little while and then heard men singing. I didn't believe the stories of men singing while waiting to be picked up, but there was a vessel nearby called Daisy and the men were singing 'Daisy, Daisy'. It was extraordinary.

Another incredible experience by a Bath naval man occurred just before Christmas 1939, as he became involved in one of the most dramatic episodes of the war so far. The Battle of the River Plate was the first major naval engagement and took place in the South Atlantic off the coast of Uruguay, which at the time was neutral. The initial clash was between the German 'pocket battleship' *Admiral Graf Spee* and three British cruisers, HMS *Exeter, Ajax* and *Achilles*. Although *Exeter* was severely crippled, the two accompanying cruisers, along with the *Graf Spee*, incurred only moderate damage. However, in the case of the latter this proved critical, as it was the fuel system which had been hit. Taking refuge in the port of Montevideo, the Uruguayan capital, the German captain ultimately scuttled his ship; although not before releasing the British prisoners it had aboard. These included Captain Charles Pottinger of 6, Fox Hill, Combe Down, Bath, who had been in charge of the SS *Ashlea* when it had been 'captured' and destroyed (once the crew were taken off) by the German ship. Captain Pottinger and the other British prisoners were still on the *Graf Spee* when the naval battle took place and, like Reginald Turner before him, he later recounted his experience to the *Bath Chronicle*:

> We couldn't grumble about the way we were treated in the Graf Spee. Mostly we played rummy and sat around and smoked. The Germans let us keep our money and we bought cigarettes from their ship's stores. We were well fed, well quartered, and I've no complaints. We were locked in during the battle, naturally. It was strange down there during the firing, but the men kept their spirits up and sang 'Sweet Adeline' and 'Pack Up your Troubles'.

A film version of the episode produced the following year entitled *For Freedom* saw Captain Pottinger playing himself on the big screen. When the film played at the Odeon cinema in Bath, Mrs Pottinger was in attendance and the picture, according to the *Bath Chronicle*, 'aroused a considerable amount of excitement in the audience'.

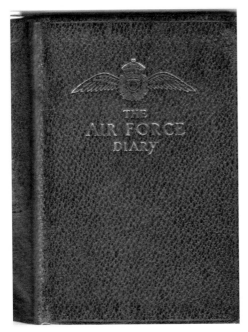

RAF diary belonging to the authors' grandfather, Ernest Lassman

Entries from 1943 RAF diary belonging to authors' grandfather.

Throughout the war, writing once again became a key element in both the recording of experiences by individuals or groups, whether through diaries and journals, or else one of the main means of communication between those abroad fighting and their loved ones left behind. As in World War One, however, letters would be censored if the authorities felt too much information was being given away.

On 10 May 1940, Hitler finally made his move, by invading France and the Low Countries, and the 'Phoney War' ended. From the start of Germany's expansion westward, the number of Bath men killed in action began to rise significantly. Although local men had died serving in all the forces, from almost the beginning of the war, for those serving on land or in the air, any casualties which had been endured resulted not from enemy engagement, as at sea, but through illness or accidents. Wallace Southerton RAFVC died in October 1939, Private Sydney J. Calley of the 4th Battalion Somerset Light Infantry died in January 1940, and Lance Corporal William Manns the following month. The deaths of Kenneth Sherman and recently married Percy Frederick Harold Thurgar, a 23-year-old sergeant in No.87 RAF Squadron, which took place in October 1939 and February 1940, were the result of air accidents; both men were serving in the RAF.

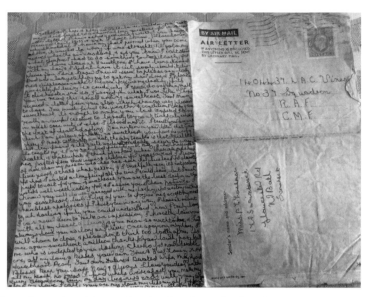

A letter from the authors' Auntie Pearl to her future husband, George Vines, while he was serving abroad.

Lance Corporal William Roy Manns, 8th Battalion of the Worcestershire Regiment, of 55, First Avenue, Oldfield Park, who died on 2 February 1940, became, despite dying of an illness, technically the first military (as opposed to naval) casualty of the war, having been on active service in France for three weeks. (Private Calley, 34, had still been training in England when he succumbed to his illness-related death a couple of weeks earlier.) Manns' parents requested that his body be repatriated for burial, back in his home city of Bath, but the War Office were unable to accede to this request and so his funeral was held overseas. Four of his closest comrades were pall bearers, while others walked immediately behind the coffin to represent his relatives. A memorial service was held for him back in the city, at St Marks Church, Walcot, eight days after his death. During it, the vicar said that William Manns was a regular worshipper at the church and that he had actually been baptised there almost 21 years ago to the day. An only son who had been called up for service in July 1939, Manns had previously worked as a clerk at the Guildhall and Basil Ogden, the town clerk, was one of the mourners. The average age of all those who died in the war would be 26; Manns had celebrated his 21st birthday the day before he had set off for France, three weeks before his death. He may have been the first military casualty on active service, but with Hitler now on the move, he certainly would not be the last.

Throughout the Second World War many new weapons were designed and developed by the various Admiralty departments evacuated to Bath in

September 1939. One of these departments was the Director of Naval Land Equipment (DNLE), which had taken up residency in the Grand Pump Room Hotel in Stall Street.

One of the projects DNLE worked on was the 'Cultivator No.6'. This was a pet project of Winston Churchill (at the time still First Lord of the Admiralty) who had been appalled at the high number of casualties on the western front during the previous war and demanded a means of allowing infantry to approach the enemy lines in relative safety. Cultivator No.6, nicknamed 'Nellie' after part of the department's initials, was a trench-cutting machine intended to work its way across no man's land towards the enemy with the infantry following in its wake. By the end of the 1939, a working model of the machine had been produced, but this was as far as the project would progress. If the First World War – at least on the western front – had become synonymous with stalemate and entrenchment, then speed and ease of movement came to epitomise the early stages of Hitler's invasion of France and the Low Countries, which began on 10 May 1940; projects such as Cultivator No.6 became obsolete overnight.

Germany's highly motorised war machine was able to move at lightning speeds, leading to the term 'lightning war', or in German *Blitzkrieg*, and through the spring of 1940, with nothing able to stop its momentum, several Western European countries found themselves now under German rule. Denmark and Norway had been first, during April; now followed Belgium and Holland, starting on 10 May.

Like their predecessors in the First World War, the British Expeditionary Force had arrived in France with high hopes but, just as before, any early success was swiftly wiped out by retreat, defeat and high casualty rates. This time, the BEF was part of the resources commanded by the French commander in chief General Gamelin. His plan was simple. When (rather than if) a German attack came, the imposing French defensive Maginot Line would more than likely divert it through Belgium. Gamelin would then rush his best troops, including the BEF, toward that area, where they would hold back the Germans along the River Dyle. On 11 May, the day after Hitler put his planned invasion into action, the BEF duly arrived at its intended position along the river bank. But the Allied defenders were outsmarted and outmanoeuvred. The German attack came further south and the speed at which it was executed took everyone by surprise.

Three days later, on the 14th, a German force did appear on the opposite bank of the Dyle and fierce fighting began. In 1918, the BEF was the best fighting machine in the world, but during the interwar period defence cuts had pared it back to the point where most of its troops, although abundant in enthusiasm, lacked experience. On 17 May, the BEF withdrew and by the next night had reached its reserve force dug in along the River Escaut, deeper into Belgium. From here, the leader of the BEF, Lord Gort, ordered a counter-attack near Arras. After some initial success, the momentum stalled, and they once again withdrew, this time to the Franco-Belgian border, arriving there on 22 May. The following day, Lord Gort ordered his troops to draw back towards the French port of Dunkirk, a decision that ultimately saved the BEF from complete annihilation.

For the men of Bath, the chances of survival were greater if you belonged to the 3rd Division of the BEF, commanded by up-and-coming General Bernard 'Monty' Montgomery. Anticipating what was going to happen, he had trained his division in conducting an orderly retreat. The rest of the BEF had done little if any training, and as so many soldiers had no previous military experience, when the Germans attacked there was chaos.

Operation Dynamo, the evacuation of the British Expeditionary Force from Dunkirk, took place between 26 May and 4 June 1940. Although in military terms it was a complete disaster – equipment, ammunition and transport were abandoned, countless men lost their lives, and the main objective the BEF had been sent over to France for had failed miserably – it nevertheless quickly attained mythic status in the eyes of the British public. A small armada of marine craft of all shapes, sizes and descriptions – naval, merchant, civilian and private – made their way across the English Channel, again and again, under heavy fire, to ultimately rescue more than 338,000 British (and French) soldiers from the clutches of the approaching German army.

Bath men were on either side of the operation, so to speak, both as rescuers and the rescued. Not everyone managed to be evacuated: many died on the beaches or were simply not seen again once the rescue crafts had left. Among those reported missing was Company Sergeant Major Reginald Pritchard of the 2nd Wiltshire Regiment. The eldest son of Mrs F. Cannings of 11, Clement Street, Bath, he was the brother of Ronald Pritchard, one of the men who lost their lives when HMS *Courageous* was sunk back in 1939. Educated at Walcot Parochial School, he had been in the army for fifteen years and served many of those years abroad. A few months later it emerged he had been taken prisoner and was being held at a camp in Germany. During those months when there was no news, parishioners at his local church had, most likely, offered prayers for his safe return.

A further cause for concern and prayers of the Walcot parishioners was the 'disappearance' of Reverend Edward William Gedge, a former curate of the parish but now a forces chaplain. He was reportedly seen wounded on the Dunkirk beach, according to the *Bath Chronicle,* having previously been transferred to a field ambulance corps and later to a main dressing station, but not sighted since. Reverend Gedge had been Walcot curate for several years back in the 1920s but had left Bath in 1928. After holding a number of different posts, he became chaplain to the Royal Engineers after the outbreak of war. As concerns for his fate grew, it transpired he had not been wounded at all but rather was helping those that were; at least this was according to the soldier who came forward to say his last sighting of the reverend, as he (the soldier) was being evacuated, was of the clergyman standing on the shore making sure everyone got off safely. As heart-warming and hopeful as this scene sounded, it still did not account for what had happened to him since then. It would be several months before the truth about the reverend's fate became known: that he too had been captured by the Germans and like Reginald Pritchard was a prisoner of war and so would, God willing, return safely to Bath at war's end.

Another former curate from Walcot, Reverend Benjamin G.B. Fox, was reported as missing by the War Office on the last day of the evacuation, but after relatives received a postcard from him postmarked the 5th of June – the day after – hope of him being safe was renewed. This indeed was the case and towards the end of the month it could be reported that Reverend Fox had returned to Bath, 'in good health, although, naturally, tired and shaken up'.

Sadly though, there were many men from Bath who would never make it back from France at all, having either died at Dunkirk or during the BEF's short-lived campaign before it. These included 26-year-old Samuel A. Arthurs, who was killed on the first day of Hitler's 'invasion'. A private in the 2nd Battalion of the Gloucestershire Regiment, Arthurs came from the Whiteway area of Bath. He is commemorated on the Dunkirk Memorial which is at Nord, France, and was unveiled on 29 June 1957 by Her Majesty Queen Elizabeth, the Queen Mother. It commemorates the 4,513 service personnel who were known to have died during the evacuation but who have no known grave.

On Monday, 27 May, the evacuation from Dunkirk began and the following morning Belgium, by order of its King, surrendered. On Tuesday the 28th, 32-year-old Captain James M.T. Ritchie of the 1st Battalion Oxfordshire & Buckinghamshire Light Infantry died; he lies in the Hazebrouck Communal Cemetery in France. The next day John Robert Featherstone, a 26-year-old gunner in the 226th Anti-Tank Battery of the 57th Regiment Royal Artillery died, as did George Gilbert, a private in the 164th Field Ambulance of the Royal Army Medical Corps. Gilbert is buried in Hoogstade Churchyard, while Featherstone is commemorated on the Dunkirk Memorial.

And still the deaths of Bath men continued. Thursday, 30 May, saw Claude Lionel Gray killed. Gray was a lance corporal in the Royal Army Ordnance Corps and is buried in St James's cemetery in Dover. He was the husband of Violet G. Gray of Fairfield Park. The last day of the month saw the deaths of Arthur John

Lewis and Albert Percy Wright. Lewis was a driver in the Royal Army Service Corps and is buried in De Panne Communal Cemetery in Belgium; Wright was a 28-year-old sergeant in the 3rd RAMC Casualty Clearing Station. He was the son of Joseph and Ethel Wright of Bathwick and is remembered on the Dunkirk Memorial.

On 14 May, Pilot Officer Peter William Vaughan of No.4 Squadron RAF died. He is buried in the Outgaarden Communal Cemetery; located at Vlaams-Brabant, about 52km south-east of Brussels. And then on the first day of the evacuation, James Henderson Deas, a 21-year-old pilot officer from No.26 Squadron was killed in action (although he was initially reported as missing). He was the son of James and Minnie Deas of Bath and lies in the Calais Southern Cemetery. He had been serving with his squadron in France since early April. At the outbreak of the war he was a flight cadet and towards the end of the previous year had been gazetted to the RAF with a permanent commission. He was an Old Edwardian and his father had served in the previous war as a flight lieutenant in the Royal Flying Corps.

Edward William F. Maggs, aged 27, a sergeant in the 1st Grenadier Guards, was killed on 1 June – his name appears on the Dunkirk Memorial – but by the time the Operation Dynamo had finished three days later, 338,000 men had been rescued and were now back in England, most ready to fight another day.

That is not to say everything was plain sailing for those who managed to get back to England, as there was, in several cases, tragedy waiting. Lance Corporal Harry George Sweet, for example, was a military policeman recently evacuated with the BEF from Dunkirk. He was travelling to Bath to visit his wife who was staying with a sister in Odd Down. Making his way through nearby Frome, Lance Corporal Sweet was crushed by a bus in the town centre. He was taken to Bath's Royal United Hospital but subsequently died of his injuries. An inquest held in the city's Guildhall the following Wednesday returned a verdict of 'accidental death'.

Several local men belonged to a company that was a hark-back to the patriotic spirit that existed in the First World War. Then, whole streets of men had joined up together and became known as Pals Companies. Back in January of 1940 it had been announced that a General Construction Company within the Royal Engineers was being recruited in Bath and Somerset for service overseas. A company of 250 men between the ages of 20 and 55 was required and would include carpenters, draughtsmen, clerks, engine-hands, fitters and tradesmen of all classes. In charge of the company would be Colonel Stead, county surveyor for Somerset and Mr John Owens, the deputy city engineer for Bath. It became known as the Bath 'Pals' company. The *Bath Chronicle* of 1 June 1940 listed several of the 'pals', including the Williams brothers, who had been wounded:

Two brothers, sleeping side by side in France were awakened, with other members of their company – the Bath 'Pals' Constructional Company of the Royal Engineers, by the sound of Nazi aircraft diving, machine-gunning, and bombing the buildings. Both are now lying wounded in hospitals, one still in France, the other in Surrey. They are Gilbert and Leslie Williams, sons of Mrs. F. E. Williams, Homeleigh, 191, Newbridge Road, Bath. Gilbert, aged 23, is in a Surrey Hospital with a fractured shoulder and broken right arm. It is not yet known what injuries Leslie, who is twenty years of age, has received. Mrs. Williams told a representative of this paper that she had been to see Gilbert and found him very ill. Both are carpenters by trade *[and they]* joined up together in February.

Other 'Pals' mentioned included Sappers James Naish of Combe Down, William Archer of Kingston Buildings, and Percy Plackman who had been working at Fortts in Milsom Street as a waiter when he joined the company in February. In the report on Naish, the newspaper mentioned another Combe Down sapper – A.E. Payton – who had been killed.

There were happy endings as well for those who made it back from France. During a 48-hour furlough, following his return from Dunkirk, Frank Davis, a gunner in the Royal Artillery, married Miss May Jones at Rush Hill Congregational Church. The bride was the eldest daughter of Mr & Mrs Jones of Luther Cottage, Odd Down, while the groom was the elder son of Mr and Mrs F. Davis, of nearby 1, Bristol View, Odd Down. The best man was the groom's brother who was serving in the RAF but had no doubt also been given leave. A reception was held afterwards at the bride's home, but due to the groom's imminent return to his regiment, any honeymoon was put on hold indefinitely.

CHAPTER 3

Valour, Defence & Espionage
(June 1940)

Although the German war machine had seemed unstoppable as it blitzkrieged its way through the Low Countries and then France back in May, they did not have it completely their own way and several heroic acts were performed, one of which was by a Bath man.

Bath's official memorial to its wartime dead stands at one of the many entrances to Royal Victoria Park; the most southerly one, in sight of nearby Queen Square. Of all the hundreds of names on the monument, only one has VC engraved after it. The two letters stand for Victoria Cross, which is the most prestigious medal that can be awarded to those serving in the British and Commonwealth forces.

Bath's official war memorial at the entrance to Royal Victoria Park

The VC was established by Queen Victoria in 1856 but made retrospective to June 1854 to cover the recent Crimean War. From that conflict onwards, it had been awarded to those who showed the 'most conspicuous bravery, or some daring or pre-eminent act of valour or self-sacrifice, or extreme devotion to duty in the presence of the enemy'.

Sergeant Thomas Gray was an RAF observer whose actions on Sunday, 12 May 1940, were deemed worthy of this highest honour. Gray was awarded the VC along with Flying Officer Donald Garland, the pilot of the Fairey Battle aircraft they were in. The German invasion of France and the Low Countries had begun at dawn on 10 May 1940. Two days later, Gray, Garland and another crew member were in the lead aircraft of a formation of five, on a mission to destroy (at all costs) the still intact Veldwezelt Bridge located over the Albert canal that was allowing German troops to advance into Belgium. All those on the mission were volunteers and the five crew had been selected through drawing lots (as all the air crews in the squadron had volunteered for the operation). Intense machine-gun and anti-aircraft fire was waiting for the crews of No.12 Squadron as they flew in at low altitude to deliver their dive-bombing attack, while at the same time they also had to contend with enemy fighters. They were successful in their objective, but only one of the five aircraft returned safely, the others, including the crew of Gray's plane, being listed as 'missing in action'.

Within a month of the operation, on 11 June, it was announced that Gray and Garland were to receive Victoria Crosses. In the accompanying message it said that the king had conferred the awards on them 'in recognition of most conspicuous bravery'. Much of this vital operation's success was 'attributed to the formation led by Flying Officer Garland, and to the coolness and resource of Sergeant Gray, who, in the most difficult conditions, navigated Flying Officer Garland's aircraft in such a manner that the whole formation was able successfully to attack the target in spite of subsequent heavy losses.'

Four days later, the *Bath Chronicle* reported the news, to which they were sure 'admirers will thrill with pride of the supreme heroism [Gray] displayed at a vital moment during the great German drive into Belgium.'

Sergeant Thomas Gray was born in Urchfont, near Devizes in the neighbouring county of Wiltshire, but more recently had made his home in Bath, at 2 Alexandra Place, Odd Down. He had been born in 1914 and after being educated at Warminster Secondary School, entered the RAF as an apprentice at Halton, where he remained for three years. He then became a fitter, and subsequently an observer, having been made a sergeant two years earlier. The *Bath Chronicle* reported that on the outbreak of war he had gone to France with his squadron and had taken part in reconnaissance flights over the Siegfried Line and into Germany.

The newspaper also relayed that Gray had last been home on leave in January [1940] and 'he was looking forward to coming home again shortly to get married to Miss Zoe Sedman of Driffield, Yorks. He mentioned this fact in a letter which his parents received only a day or two before he was posted missing.' He 'would have been home earlier but for the fact that he gave up his leave to another airman to enable him to come home to see his wife and baby.' Gray had met his fiancée when he had been stationed near her Yorkshire home.

On the following Monday, the Mayor of Bath (Dr J.S. Carpenter) called on Mr and Mrs Gray to express his congratulations on the honour bestowed upon their son and the hope that they would soon have happy tidings of his whereabouts.

Sergeant Gray's father had been born at Colerne and served twenty-six years in the Wiltshire Police before retiring and coming to live in Bath. He retired with the rank of sergeant and his last station was at Horningsham. Mrs Gray was a Londoner. The newspaper listed Thomas Gray's six siblings, several of whom were, like their now distinguished brother, serving in the armed forces. Two of whom, Arthur, aged 28, and Reginald, 21, were corporals in the RAF; the former was on HMS *Courageous* when she sank but was among those saved. A third brother followed in his father's footsteps and had joined the Wiltshire Police – having previously served in the Life Guards. The fourth was a transport driver, the fifth engaged on munitions work, and the youngest of Thomas's brothers was still at school.

Despite the belief of Gray's fiancée that 'I am sure . . . he is alive and well, and that I shall hear from him soon,' Gray and the other crew members had been killed during the mission; which meant the VCs had been awarded posthumously.

Controversially, the third member of the crew – Leading Aircraftman L.R. Reynolds – did not receive the honour, as he was judged not to have been in a decision-making position.

Despite this act of bravery and the loss of life by the RAF, the Germans found their way through and after securing the rest of the Low Countries marched into France. By the middle of June 1940 victorious German troops had marched down the Champs-Elysées and a few days later France surrendered. On the 21st of the month the French signed an armistice agreement in the same railway carriage the Germans had signed the one bringing an end to the First World War two decades earlier. Hitler subsequently ordered the carriage to be burnt. Lessons had obviously been learnt from the earlier conflict, as it had taken this German army just seventeen days to accomplish what their predecessors had spent four and a half years trying and ultimately failing to achieve.

In May 1940, as Hitler had begun his march westward, Winston Churchill had succeeded Neville Chamberlain as British prime minister. Now, with France under German occupation, it was a distinct possibility Britain would be next and with thoughts of invasion uppermost in his mind, Churchill gave his famous 'Their Finest Hour' speech, in which he solemnly announced to the British people that 'The Battle of France is over, I expect that the Battle of Britain is about to begin.' With this speech, along with many others, Churchill became, as he later put it, the 'roar' of a nation with the determination to do whatever was required to defeat Hitler.

In the middle of May 1940, Secretary of State for War Anthony Eden had made a call for volunteers to form a new force – to be known as LDV. Although during its brief existence it would unofficially become known as 'Look, Duck and Vanish', its official title was the 'Local Defence Volunteers'. The day after the announcement, a quarter of a million men registered at their local police stations and by the time the organisation's name was changed to the Home Guard, two months later, more than a million had joined its ranks. In Bath, 600 men initially responded to Eden's call to arms, and this would ultimately rise to more than 2,500 throughout the city, along with 200 female auxiliaries.

Although from our present-day perspective we laugh at the antics of this 'Dad's Army', the reality is that they would have been the first and, in many cases, only line of defence against the invading German troops, whether coming by sea or air. Although many of the comic scenarios in the television series were based on real-life situations that the two creators had themselves experienced – both had been part of the Home Guard during the war – this was not an unkind or malicious send up. As it was made clear on many occasions in the series – and in interviews the show's creators gave – these men on television, like their real-life counterparts, would have laid down their lives in defence of their country.

In regard to *Dad's Army* the television series, there is a strong link between it and the city of Bath; namely the actor who played one of the main characters in the series: that of Private Godfrey. The actor was, of course, Arnold Ridley, who was born in Walcot and educated at Bath City Secondary Day School. The co-educational establishment, which was the 'great, great grandfather' of present day Beechen Cliff School, according to the book *Basement to Beechen Cliff*, was founded in the same year, 1896, as this most illustrious alumnus was born and was originally located in the basement – hence the title of the book – of the Guildhall's North Wing.

During the First World War the future actor served with the 6th Battalion Somerset Light Infantry. He was wounded during the Somme Campaign in 1916 and invalided out of the army the following year. Although physically and mentally scarred, he nevertheless volunteered for military service at the outbreak of the Second World War and became a Major of Intelligence with the British

Expeditionary Force. He was discharged from military service on medical grounds, having suffered acute shell shock. Although most widely known for his portrayal of the elderly Private Godfrey, Arnold Ridley was also the author of the 1923 play *The Ghost Train* (later a film starring Arthur Askey) and played Doughy Hood in *The Archers*.

When it was first formed in May 1940, the Somerset Home Guard consisted of ten battalions (three more would be added in 1943) spread throughout the county, two of which were based in Bath. The first was designated the 5th Somerset (Bath City) Battalion, consisting of local men and with its headquarters at 15 Queen Square, while the other, with Admiralty personnel, was the 6th Somerset (Bath Admiralty) Battalion. Each battalion was allowed a paid Civilian Administrative Officer, as well as a Gas Officer, although thankfully gas was never used during this war.

The Bath City Battalion, originally under the command of Colonel G.H. Rogers OBE DL (then later Lieutenant Colonel L.R.E.W. Taylor DSO), consisted of nine companies, which included the Headquarters Company based in Monmouth Place. Of the remaining eight, six covered the suburbs and two the city centre itself. Those covering the outskirts were: No.1 (South-east), No.2 (North-east), No.3 (North-west), No.4 (South-west), No.5 (South) and No.6 (North-east). Although No.2 and No.6 were both named North-east, the former covered the Larkhall and Swainswick areas, while the latter Batheaston and Northend. The 7th Company covered the city centre, as did the 8th, the 'Works' Company, consisting mainly of employees from the various utility companies, including a platoon solely made up of Stothert & Pitt employees.

Other employers in the city helped form battalions based outside the county. The Post Office, for example, formed what became the 15th Gloucester (Post Office) Battalion, of which a platoon within 'A' Company was located in Bath, and the Southern Railway had several battalions of which one was the 22nd Devon (5th Southern Railway) Battalion. Employees of the Somerset and Dorset Line within the city were expected to join its 'E' company, which covered Bath and Templecombe.

Although the Home Guard would eventually become a fully trained fighting force, whose numbers equalled that of the actual army, to begin with, weapons, uniforms and other necessary equipment required to fight the Germans would be sadly lacking. Pitchforks and home-made weapons, along with armbands, would be the order of the day. The companies on the edge of the city, especially the north-east ones, were fairly lucky in so much as many of their members already owned firearms, usually shotguns. It was soon found these guns could be made more lethal by pouring wax into the cartridge to prevent the shot from spreading.

A pre-uniformed 'C' Platoon of No.4 Company.

The Home Guard on the Recreation Ground, Bath.

The firm of Eley, which made the cartridges for these guns, even took up the idea and began producing cartridges with a single solid ball rather than multiple shot. This shortage of weapons would be rectified when a large detachment of machine guns arrived from America (which had supposedly been captured by the FBI from gangsters) and at some point during the war, several Bath Home Guard companies would be issued with a Lewis Gun, a type of light machine gun.

Also based in Bath was the 6th Somerset (Bath Admiralty) Battalion of the Home Guard. Its headquarters was initially in Edward Street (and Holburne Museum) but would eventually move to the Empire Hotel. Its companies covered the main Admiralty sites around Bath: 'A' Company being at Foxhill, 'B' Company at Ensleigh, 'C' Company the city centre offices, and 'D' Company at Warminster Road. The remaining one was 'E' (Anti-aircraft) Company. The sites covered by A, B and D companies were the large areas of recently built hutments, which were to serve as more permanent workplaces for the Admiralty departments, rather than their temporary hotel-based ones.

The battalion's commanding officer was Commander D.C. Morrison RN (Retired). The 6th Battalion had an immediate advantage over the 5th in that they had access to Naval Stores and were thus far better equipped. The battalion also possessed old Maxim machine guns from the Great War and assorted types of rifle of various vintages. They were also accorded the honour of being inspected, on the Recreation Ground, by Lord Louis Mountbatten.

All Home Guard companies underwent training and were expected to learn such German expressions as 'hande hoch' (hands up), 'waffen hinlegen' (throw down your weapons), and 'ergebt euch' (surrender). Whether this was, in retrospect, a wise move is open to question, as calling out into the darkness in German might well have led

The Odd Down Company of the 5th Somerset (Bath City) Battalion Home Guard.

to tragic consequences. One tragedy that did happen, although it had nothing to do with German expressions, occurred later that summer.

On Saturday, 17 August 1940, the 5th Somerset (Bath City) Battalion of the Home Guard suffered what is believed to be their first fatality of the war. The circumstances surrounding the man's death though, at least to anyone reading the *Bath Chronicle*'s account of the incident, seemed very odd indeed. Under the headline 'Two Men Killed in Field Near Bath', it reported that 'As the result of an accident which occurred at Charmy Down, near Swainswick, Bath,

Henry Pickford with his daughter Marianne.

at a quarter to six on Saturday morning, two men received injuries which were immediately fatal. It is believed they were talking together in a field at the time.' The two victims were named as Henry Charles Pickford, of Tadwick Farm, Upper Swainswick and Albert William Simmonds, a lorry driver of West Hoathly, Sussex, who had been living in a caravan near Swainswick. No inquest, it added, would be held in either case. The report mentioned that Henry, or Harry as he was known locally, Pickford was an enthusiastic member of the local Home Guard, belonging to No.2 (North-east) Company of the 5th Somerset (Bath City) Battalion. Accordingly, at his funeral, which took place at St Mary Magdalene Church at Langridge, more than fifty members of the company, as well as the commanding officer of the whole Bath Battalion, Colonel Guy Rogers, were in attendance.

Harry Pickford was the only son of George Pickford and grew up on Manor Farm, in the tiny hamlet of Langridge, but had moved to Tadwick Farm when he married Miss Edith Ann Harrill of Corston six years previously. According to the *Bath Chronicle,* he was 'a very popular and well-known man in the district' and as soon as volunteers had been called for to join the LDV he had registered. As well as his widow, he left a 4-year-old daughter, Marianne, who would for weeks after her father's death, according to Jeffery Wilson in his exhaustive book on the Somerset Home Guard, wait patiently at the cottage window every evening for her father to return home.

Albert Simmons left a widow and two children, aged 4 and 7. They were living with him in the caravan, having arrived in Bath three weeks before, so as to be with him while he was working away, and were treating it as a holiday.

The truth, as probably all those attending the funeral knew, was that Harry Pickford and Albert Simmonds had been killed by an unexploded bomb, which had been dropped by a German bomber earlier in the week on the still-under-construction RAF Charmy Down. The airfield was being built at a location north of Swainswick, between the Langridge and St Catherine's areas on the north-east outskirts of Bath and it was part of the duties of No.2 (North-east) Company to guard it; Simmonds was most likely there in his professional capacity as a driver.

Although there were no witnesses to the incident, it is believed that having placed his rifle and dog in his car, before going off duty and home, Harry Pickford returned to the vicinity of an unexploded bomb. Possibly the two men were trying to move the bomb, or else defuse it, but whatever took place on that Saturday, suddenly the tranquillity of the early hours was shattered by a violent explosion, killing Harry and Albert. Investigation showed a large crater and the bodies of the two men, who had most likely been killed instantly.

The 'vagueness' of the reporting, which lent it a strange, even sinister tone, was obviously down to reporting censorship. The newspaper could not describe

The grave of Henry Pickford at Langridge, who was killed by a bomb at Charmy Down while on duty with the 5th Somerset (Bath City) Battalion Home Guard.

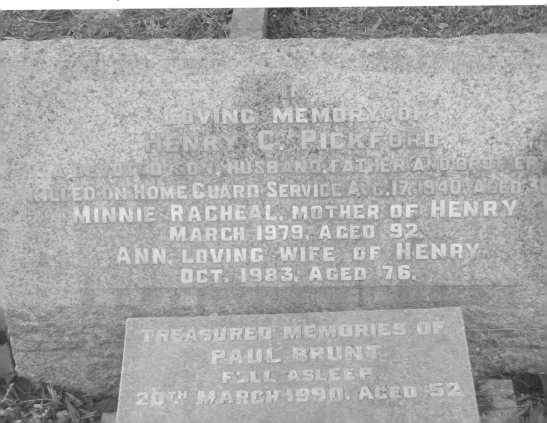

The eternal view afforded from the grave of Henry Pickford.

the nature of the 'accident', as this would have informed anyone reading the report that an airfield base was being built and allowed the Germans to assess the accuracy of their bombing. The fact that there would be no inquest on either of the men would, however, have suggested to any astute reader that these deaths were no accident but 'due to war operations', as was the well-worn euphemism. This was the 5th Somerset (Bath City) Battalion's first loss of life, but Harry Pickford's death would not be their last.

With the intention of impeding the enemy's movement across the country, a defence system known as 'stop lines' began to be erected. 'GHQ Stop Lines', as they were officially called, were a series of fixed defences which would run across southern Britain and each was named after a colour. Stop Line 'White' ran from Bridgwater Bay to Lyme Bay, but was also known as the Taunton Stop Line, 'Green' was located between Gloucester and Bridgwater Bay facing west before turning east along Wellow Valley to Freshford facing south, while 'Yellow' ran from Freshford to Frome.

As part of these defences, there were several pillboxes located near Bath. The first (Grid Ref. ST739676) guarded the Admiralty hutments at Ensleigh, while another (Grid Ref. ST798676) overlooked the railway siding at Monkton Farleigh Ammunition Depot, east of Bathford.

The stop line scheme was never completely finished, since part way through construction a new policy was adopted: of having a central reserve that could move to wherever landings were taking place. One reason for this, no doubt, was that it had been realised that the stop lines, intended to impede the enemy, could easily impede our own forces instead.

In addition to these other preparations, an organisation was created which was so top secret that only in the last few years has its existence become widely known. Even today, the researcher aiming to delve into its structure, activities and personnel often finds himself entering a web of mystery and misinformation, where details can be, at best, incomplete or even contradictory. What is for certain, however, is that during this summer of 1940, with Hitler poised across the water, the government instigated a British resistance organisation. This consisted of what were known as Auxiliary Units, whose purpose if a successful invasion happened was to do everything they could to harass the enemy, such as blocking roads, setting booby traps and destroying food stocks. It is not surprising, perhaps, to learn that the life expectancy of any auxiliary called into action was around twelve days.

These stay-behind groups were set up across the length and breadth of Britain and consisted of around 6,000 auxiliaries nationwide, all enlisted from reserved occupations. Each unit was designated a number and title of 'GHQ Reserve'. The Bath unit was officially '203rd GHQ Reserve' and its members were also enlisted in either the 5th or 6th Somerset Battalions as this would afford them protection under the Geneva Convention. Each unit was split up into groups, or patrols, and, given the secret nature of the organisation, and in case of capture by the enemy, it is unlikely that most members of the Bath patrols knew the identities of fellow auxiliaries in other units.

The Bath patrols, as far as can be ascertained, consisted of five groups that had operational bases located in the following areas: Bathampton, Englishcombe, Swainswick, South Stoke and Weston. The operational bases were where its members would go to ground in the event of invasion. From here they would carry out their clandestine activities, such as sabotage and, it has been suggested, assassination. There would also be a hidden 'explosive' dump nearby containing all the elements necessary for making home-made bombs.

The Bathampton patrol had their operational base at Hampton Rocks, in one of the old stone mines. Measures where taken to camouflage it – a specially cut stone slab which could be moved from either inside or out was placed in front of the entrance – and a living area was constructed within the cavern. In the event of invasion, the patrol's primary objectives were the railway junctions at Bathampton and Claverton Manor.

This photo is believed to show the Swainswick Auxiliary Unit. They were attached to their relevant Home Guard platoon as protection under the Geneva Convention.

The number of arms and explosives assembled by the patrols would generally be dependent on the resourcefulness of its members. One Bath patrol, not long after its formation, had acquired the following arsenal: several Smith & Wesson pistols, two P17 rifles, fighting knives and an impressive array of gelignite, sticky bombs, grenades and plastic explosives, along with detonators and time-delay fuses.

The Admiralty had five (possibly six) of its own patrols. The five known to have existed were No.1 Patrol based in Kelston Park, No.2 at Langridge, No.3 at Bathampton, No.4 within Prior Park and No.5 at Newton Park. Although auxiliaries were normally enlisted from the reserved occupations, meaning they would not be called up for service, it seems the members of the Admiralty patrols had no such protection, as the average number of men identified for most of the patrols during their existence would suggest a relatively high turnover.

Given the threat of invasion and extended range into southern England of the *Luftwaffe*'s bombing capability, from recently captured French airfields, previous contingency plans had to be swiftly revised. It wasn't just civilians and human resources which the government needed to keep safe, but also non-human resources: raw materials, munitions, equipment and even national treasures. Ammunition stores and valuable works of arts had hitherto been kept above ground, in various facilities and country houses that were deemed 'safe'. These latest developments in the war meant the government was forced to seek places below the surface with sufficient amounts of rock above – 'overburden' – to absorb any bomb blast. The high ground east of Bath, between Bathford and Corsham, had long been exploited for its fine building stone. During the 1930s many of these old quarries were converted to house not just munitions, but factories, offices and museum repositories as well. These secret underground cities provided many jobs for the locals – as well as for numerous Irish labourers – with convoys of buses and lorries taking the workers to and from the facilities every day.

Preparations were made to move certain items out of the country altogether. When it became apparent that Britain might be invaded, the government ordered financial assets, such as share certificates, bonds, and gold, to be transported to Canada. This happened during June and July 1940 under the code-name Operation Fish; so secret was it that the authorisation for it was not officially published until after the operation had been completed. The first most people in Bath knew of this was when they tried to retrieve their assets, only to be told the truth by bank staff.

For most of the war, however, financial matters were more about saving to help the war effort rather than withdrawing, and various schemes were initiated to encourage men, women and children to do so. So enthusiastic did Bath citizens become regarding this that by the end of summer 1940 Bath led the way in the National Savings scheme and three years into the war its 70,000 or so population had managed to put aside more than £3.5 million.

Apart from the national schemes, the city also had its own initiatives. Bath 'Warship Week' was one of these and was launched (no pun intended) on 21 November 1942. Again, the city rose magnificently to the task and raised nearly half of the £750,000 target in the first three days and 'adopted' the Royal Navy warship HMS *Jervis* – a 'J' Class fleet destroyer. Through the same scheme, the rural district of Bathavon adopted a 'Hunt' Class escort destroyer, HMS *Beaufort*. Both ships would survive the war.

Faced with the possibility of German troops being deposited in Britain by various means, the government ordered local authorities to remove, or deface, anything which might help them to find their way around the country. Many signs within the city and the surrounding area were removed altogether, while

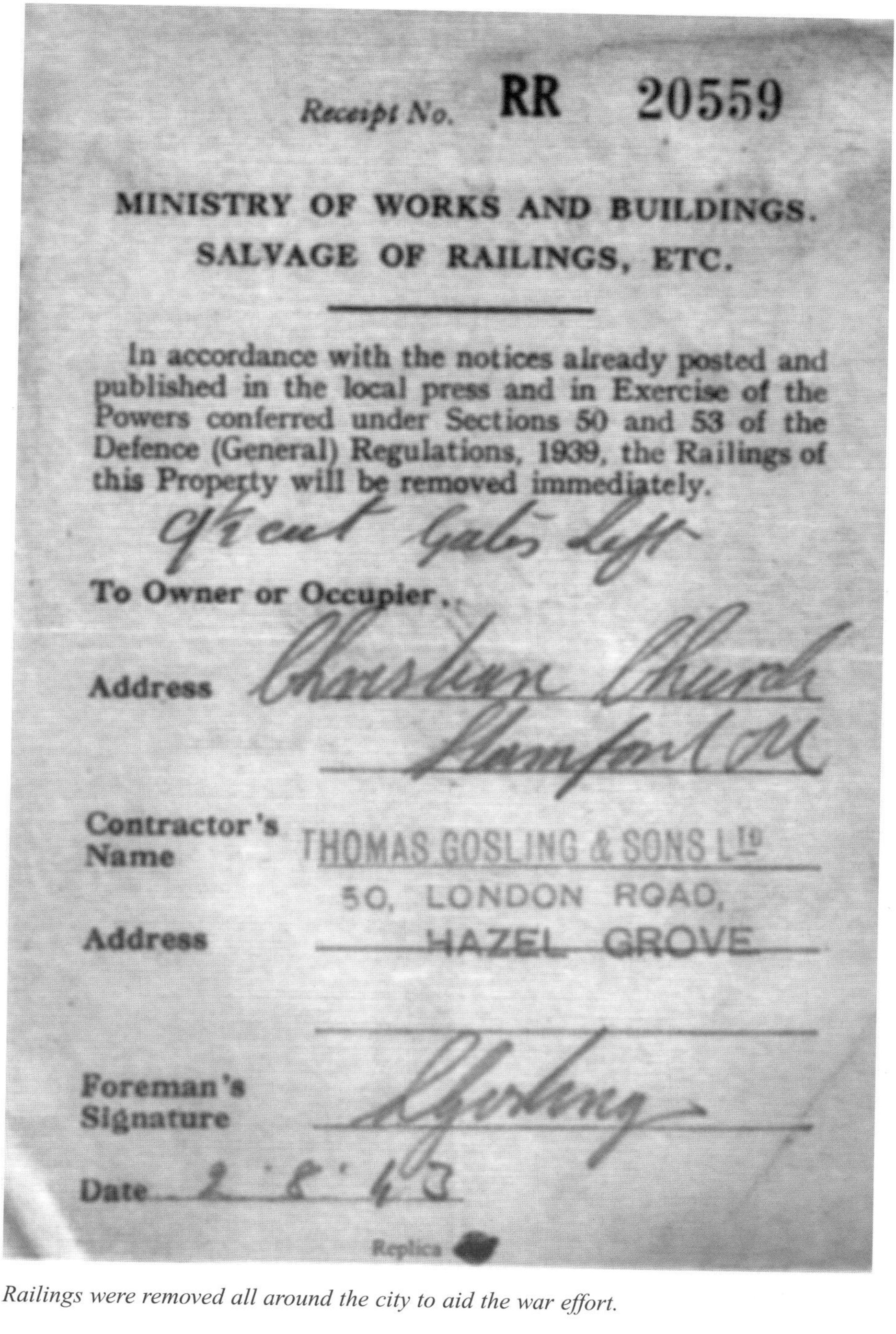

Receipt No. **RR   20559**

MINISTRY OF WORKS AND BUILDINGS.
SALVAGE OF RAILINGS, ETC.

In accordance with the notices already posted and published in the local press and in Exercise of the Powers conferred under Sections 50 and 53 of the Defence (General) Regulations, 1939, the Railings of this Property will be removed immediately.

Gt cut Gates left

To Owner or Occupier

Address *Christian Church Stamford St*

Contractor's
Name   THOMAS GOSLING & SONS Ltd

50, LONDON ROAD,

Address   HAZEL GROVE

Foreman's
Signature   *Gosling*

Date   *2 · 8 · 43*

Replica

Railings were removed all around the city to aid the war effort.

Issued by the Ministry of Information   *in co-operation with the War Office*
and the Ministry of Home Security.

If the

INVADER

comes

WHAT TO DO — AND HOW TO DO IT

THE Germans threaten to invade Great Britain. If they do so they will be driven out by our Navy, our Army and our Air Force. Yet the ordinary men and women of the civilian population will also have their part to play. Hitler's invasions of Poland, Holland and Belgium were greatly helped by the fact that the civilian population was taken by surprise. They did not know what to do when the moment came. *You must not be taken by surprise.* This leaflet tells you what general line you should take. More detailed instructions will be given you when the danger comes nearer. Meanwhile, read these instructions carefully and be prepared to carry them out.

I

When Holland and Belgium were invaded, the civilian population fled from their homes. They crowded on the roads, in cars, in carts, on bicycles and on foot, and so helped the enemy by preventing their own armies from advancing against the invaders. You must not allow that to happen here. Your first rule, therefore, is :—

(1) IF THE GERMANS COME, BY PARACHUTE, AEROPLANE OR SHIP, YOU MUST REMAIN WHERE YOU ARE. THE ORDER IS " STAY PUT ".

If the Commander in Chief decides that the place where you live must be evacuated, he will tell you when and how to leave. Until you receive such orders you must remain where you are. If you run away, you will be exposed to far greater danger because you will be machine-gunned from the air as were civilians in Holland and Belgium, and you will also block the roads by which our own armies will advance to turn the Germans out.

II

There is another method which the Germans adopt in their invasion. They make use of the civilian population in order to create confusion and panic. They spread false rumours and issue false instructions. In order to prevent this, you should obey the second rule, which is as follows :—

(2) DO NOT BELIEVE RUMOURS AND DO NOT SPREAD THEM. WHEN YOU RECEIVE AN ORDER, MAKE QUITE SURE THAT IT IS A TRUE ORDER AND NOT A FAKED ORDER. MOST OF YOU KNOW YOUR POLICEMEN AND YOUR A.R.P. WARDENS BY SIGHT, YOU CAN TRUST THEM. IF YOU KEEP YOUR HEADS, YOU CAN ALSO TELL WHETHER A MILITARY OFFICER IS REALLY BRITISH OR ONLY PRETENDING TO BE SO. IF IN DOUBT ASK THE POLICE-MAN OR THE A.R.P. WARDEN. USE YOUR COMMON SENSE.

Advice on what to do if the Germans invaded.

others were altered so all the 'fingers' pointed the same way. Others could only be defaced, one example being the old school at Bailbrook, north-east of the centre, where the word Bailbrook was filled in with cement.

Whether these measures would have confused the German troops we will never know, but they certainly did the Allied forces who found themselves stationed nearby during the war. At the same time though, these precautions were part of a larger strategy meant to deny any German spies or fifth columnists potentially useful information.

The term 'fifth columnist' had only recently entered the wartime vocabulary, having been coined during the Spanish Civil War (1936-9). It referred to the members of collaborationist groups that were native to one country but working for another. 'I have four columns advancing on Madrid,' a Spanish general is reported to have said, 'and a fifth column inside.' In the Second World War, it was known Germany already had a number of these fifth columns operating in several European countries and the fear was they were also now in England.

Two cases in which people were accused of being fifth columnists appeared in the pages of the *Bath Chronicle* during June 1940; both were women. The first was that of Olive Evelyn Baker, a former employee at the Lansdown Grove Nursing Home. When she appeared at the Bath Police Court on Monday, 10 June, the charge against her was that 'between May 14th and May 18th [1940] with intent to assist the enemy and to the prejudice of the public safety and the efficient prosecution of the war, she did unlawfully publish and distribute a number of postcards relating to enemy wireless propaganda.' In one of her correspondences to other people, as she admitted in court, she had written, 'I HAVE often seen him (Hitler) and am convinced he really was divinely sent to make the world a cleaner and better place, and the world is crucifying him.' Olive was committed for trial at the Bristol assizes, and in spite of being represented by the firm of Titley, Long, Taylor and Denning, found herself, prophetically as it turned out, on the end of a five-year sentence; meaning she would be released in 1945.

The other court case involved Lilian Ruth Yates, a 34-year-old woman of no fixed abode, who was overheard by a special constable 'condemning the British government and upholding Germany'. Material found on her person after she was apprehended was deemed to have been for unlawful purpose. Lilian Yates was defended by the same firm as Olive Baker. The bench recommended trial at the next Bristol assizes and she was given two years.

Despite the genuine danger of an 'enemy within our midst', the perceived threat sometimes produced unfounded fears and paranoia bordering on the humorous. One householder who reported their 'fifth columnist' neighbour had mistaken the dripping of a leaky cistern for the 'tap tap tapping' of enemy Morse code messages.

CHAPTER 4

Triumph and Defeat
(July 1940 – May 1941)

The Battle of Britain was not won solely in the air. Without new planes to replace those lost in aerial engagements the 'few' would simply not have been able to continue the fight. This was made possible by supreme efforts taking place on the ground – from those involved in the production of the aircraft to everyone else who contributed in some way to raising money to allow them to be built.

'Spitfire Fund' schemes began to appear around the country to raise money to build new aeroplanes. Bath's first began on 7 August 1940. It was estimated that it cost £5,000 for a new Spitfire and by the 18th, in eleven days, Bath people had reached the target. The finished aircraft, a MK1 Spitfire, was allocated the serial number X4906 and the city's crest appeared on its fuselage. It was built at the Spitfire Shadow Factory at Castle Bromwich near Birmingham in the autumn of 1940 and made its debut flight on Boxing Day that year. After initially being stationed with a nearby maintenance unit, it was transferred in June 1941 to the newly formed No.457 (Royal Australian Air Force) Squadron stationed at RAF Baginton (now Coventry airport). At some time during the war a Spitfire was displayed in the Sawclose in connection with the Spitfire Fund and this may possibly have been X4906 *City of Bath*.

In mid-August, Hitler's emphasis shifted to bombing cities, with the aim of demoralising the British people into submission and surrender. On the first day of August, Hitler changed the strategy of attacking merchant shipping and seaside towns and ordered Hermann Göring, head of the Luftwaffe, to 'overpower the English air force with all the forces at [his] command in the shortest possible time.' The start of this 'overpowering' became known as 'Eagle Day' and was set for early August. Bad weather delayed it, but once Luftwaffe crews took to the air, extensive destruction of British aircraft, airbases and associated factories began in' earnest.

The ability to target these objectives was down to the fact the Luftwaffe was able to fly from the French airfields they now controlled in the north of the country. The range of their bombers included most of southern Britain, including Bath. For the time being though, Bath was not considered to be at risk, but that would not stop its population gazing ever skyward in the coming months. There was a taste of things to come on 14 August, when the first major air battle took place over Somerset. During that afternoon the Luftwaffe attacked a number of West Country targets, including RAF Colerne over the border in Wiltshire, and the still-to-be-completed RAF Charmy Down. It is believed to be one of the bombs dropped on this day, by a Heinkel 111, but which failed to explode, that caused the deaths, a few days later, of Henry Pickford and Albert Simmonds.

Although the Luftwaffe had twice the number of aircraft as RAF Bomber Command and nearly seven times the number of trained pilots, the British had home advantage in the skies and the losses sustained by the Germans on this day, in Somerset and elsewhere, caused its commanders to return to night bombing, at least for the time being, and a series of prolonged attacks would have indirect consequences for Bath.

From mid-August, various sites and facilities around Bristol were targeted, including Filton, Avonmouth and Portishead. In early September, the emphasis of these bombing raids shifted. In retrospect, it can be seen as a blunder by Goering, as by now the RAF were close to defeat; both its pilots and planes were being lost as a rate that was not sustainable for much longer. This shift of emphasis occurred when Berlin had become the target of a British bombing raid, so infuriating the Luftwaffe's head that he decided to switch objectives and bomb England's own capital, so beginning the London Blitz.

One upshot of the London Blitz for Bath was that many of the evacuees who had left during the 'Phoney War' made a hasty return from the capital. Another consequence occurred on the first day of the bombing – 7 September 1940. As London suddenly became the target for German bombers, it was wrongly believed by the government that this was the signal for the anticipated invasion. The code-word 'Cromwell' (Invasion Imminent) was signalled throughout the country at eight o'clock that evening, alerting the Home Guard and Auxiliary Units that this was now their moment. In Bath, locals sprang into action. It is perhaps difficult for those who did not experience it to fully appreciate what it must have felt like to believe your country, your city, and your home was about to be invaded by an enemy force. Throughout the city – from Odd Down to Lansdown, from Bathwick to Swainswick – pre-arranged and well-rehearsed plans were put into action. At the Bath Home Guard headquarters, Bill Edwards, of Eden Villas in Larkhall, was told to take two men and walk to the top of Lansdown. Once there, they had orders to hold off any German troops who might try to storm the hilltop. Around the city, other Home Guard and AU personnel likewise took to strategic points overlooking the centre. After a few hours of consternation, those further up the command chain, once they realised the actual situation, cancelled the order. Thereafter, a more stringent system came into effect.

During September 1940, Hitler finally abandoned Operation Sealion, the intended invasion of England and instead focussed his attention eastwards on the invasion of Russia. At the same time, however, he gave orders for the stepping up of bombing raids, both during the night and the day, which were to be carried out against important targets on the western side of Britain.

Attacks on the West Country aircraft industry began on 25 September. One of the targets for this first bombing raid was the Bristol Aeroplane Company's plant at Filton in North Bristol. The aerial armada which appeared through the banks of cloud, giving excellent cover for its attack, consisted of Heinkel 111s, escorted by Messerschmitt 110 long-range fighters. The RAF believed that the

Bristol Aeroplane Company's works at Filton.

intended target was Yeovil, so the Luftwaffe force was able to dispatch its load pretty much unimpeded (a Heinkel 111 was shot down by men of 237 Battery, 76th HAA Regiment at Portishead). By the time they began their journey back to France though, squadrons of Spitfires and Hurricanes had been scrambled and were flying north. The British pilots intercepted the German planes above the skies of Bath and a dog-fight ensued that was no doubt a spectacle enjoyed by many watching from the city below. Although the RAF saw five of their planes downed, only one of their pilots was killed; the Luftwaffe lost four aircrew. The five British planes lost consisted of three Spitfires and two Hurricanes. One of the Hurricanes came down in a field near Mells Road Station, the other was forced to land on Charmy Down. Both pilots, from 238 Squadron based at Middle Wallop, survived. The Spitfires had come from their base in Warmell in Dorset, two of them from 152 Squadron and the third from 609 Squadron. One of the Spitfires, piloted by Sergeant J. Hugh-Rees, belly-landed near Glastonbury, while another was forced down at Newton St Loe. This latter plane was piloted by the leader of 152 Squadron, P.K. Devitt. Both Devitt and Hugh-Rees walked from the wreckage.

By now the dog-fight had moved east, and at Church Farm, Woolverton, near Frome, the third Spitfire, piloted by Sergeant K.C. Holland, crashed. It was here too that the second of the two Heinkel 111s downed in the county on that day crashed, killing all but one of its crew members. The Heinkel, pursued across the Somerset sky by several Hurricanes and Spitfires, including the one piloted by Sergeant Holland, was seriously damaged by the time it was in sight of Woolverton. But just before it crashed, as Sergeant Holland was coming in for the kill, a single shot from the Heinkel's rear gunner entered the head of the RAF man, killing him instantly. The raid on Bristol had been a heavy one, resulting in 132 people killed and 315 injured.

The first German bomb to fall within Bath's city boundaries occurred around one o'clock in the morning of 19 August. This was dropped by a Heinkel 111 on an armed reconnaissance mission and came to earth on the High Common, above what is today Victoria Park golf course. Although no lives were lost – one person was slightly injured – several of the upper windows in nearby Cavendish Crescent shattered (the lower ones being protected by a garden wall), a large crater was created, and many vegetables were destroyed in the allotments where the bomb landed. Woken by this unusual occurrence, many local people came out of their homes and walked up the hill to survey the damage.

On 24 August, five days after the High Common incident, two BSK canisters, each containing around thirty-six one kilogramme magnesium incendiary bombs, fell between the areas of Wellsway and Newbridge Hill, and on the first day of September, Newbridge Hill once again, along with areas in Twerton, were damaged by two large oil bombs and four high explosives. Four days later the Locksbrook area was the recipient of ten 50 kg high explosive bombs. Neither of these bombings caused any loss of life.

Bath was left untouched throughout October 1940, but on the evening of 24 November half a dozen high explosives landed in the Weston Park and Sion Hill areas, to be followed later that night by BSK incendiary canisters dropped across several areas of the city. In Bath there was no loss of life, but Bristol was 'heavily mauled', with the deaths of 200 Bristolians and 890 injured. Such was the intensity of the attack that fires could be seen burning up to 150 miles away.

The final bombs to fall on Bath in 1940 were on the 4 December. A solitary Heinkel 111 was on its way to Bristol, but the crew, finding unfavourable conditions, decided to drop its load – consisting of sixteen bombs – on what they believed to be 'a railway works near Bristol'. This was in fact twelve miles to the east, in the Locksbrook area of Bath. All of these bombs inexplicably failed to explode.

Seven days later, on 11 December 1940, Bath's sense of security was perhaps increased, when the first operational squadron was deployed to the recently completed airfield at RAF Charmy Down. A detachment of Hurricanes from No.87 Squadron, based across the county border at nearby RAF Colerne, had been sent to Charmy Down the previous month, but on this date the entire squadron became based at the airfield. The Hurricanes began running night-time patrols, on the lookout for German bombers, and quickly became a regular sight in the skies above the city.

Charmy Down is a plateau on the hills to the north of Bath. Steep gradients surround most of its sides, while its flat summit runs approximately two-thirds of a mile north to south and a mile east to west. It had been decided to build an airfield at the site back in 1939, and originally it was to be a satellite base for the Maintenance Unit at Colerne. When work began on its construction, however, it was built solely as a fighter base. This was because RAF Colerne had by now changed its use, being chosen as a sector station by 10 Group Fighter Command.

Once completed there would be three runways at RAF Charmy Down, the main one more than 4,000 feet long and running south-east to north-west. It had 39 aircraft dispersals consisting of 12 double fighter pens and 15 single dispersals – these were mounds of earth that would effectively shield the stationary aircraft from the outfall of exploding bombs. The control tower was located on the western side of the airfield, along with briefing rooms and operational buildings. Numerous hangers were built all around the site, including a Bellman hanger on the main technical site,

Above: The control tower at former RAF Charmy Down; one of the few remaining features still on site.

Below: The authors on a visit to the former RAF Charmy Down.

located on the site's eastern side. At its peak, more than 2,500 personnel would live and work at the airfield.

No.87 Squadron had served in France as part of the air component of the British Expeditionary Force, and had suffered heavy losses during the German invasion, as well as the earlier loss of Bath man, Sergeant Percy Thurgar, in an accident. No.87 was to become one of the longest-serving Hurricane night-fighter squadrons and by Christmas the entire squadron was at RAF Charmy Down.

Elsewhere in the city, Christmas 1940 was, by all accounts, a rather subdued affair. By now, rationing had been enforced for nearly a year and so the usual indulgent Yuletide fare was limited. The *Bath Chronicle* pondered the fact that sandwiches would probably be the mainstay of most household's parties and suggested that they 'be small and slim, and cut in different shapes, [and instead] of keeping to the conventional fillings… go out for a touch a novelty.' They offered suggestions for a quartet of sandwich spreads that used available wartime ingredients: cheese or chutney; sardine cream; banana & marmalade; or almonds & raisins.

Defences in the shape of pillboxes at the former RAF Charmy Down.

As with the previous New Year, the beginning of 1941 saw a period of extreme cold. Indeed, it was so cold that water froze as soon as it left fire hoses and hit the buildings. This was the experience of a crew from Bath Fire Service when they travelled the twelve or so miles west to neighbouring Bristol to help in the aftermath of another German bombing raid. This occurred on 3 January and was the fourth major attack on the port city.

To assist their counterparts in Bristol, who were coming under increasing pressure, fire crews from local areas, including Bath, were drafted in to provide support. Crews from Bath would continue to help during the first months of 1941, culminating in the infamous Good Friday raid of 11 April 1941. It wasn't just

So cold the water from the fire engines froze.

near neighbours that assisted: crews came from as far away as Birmingham, Manchester and Southampton to help extinguish blitz fires.

During the early January raid on Bristol, bombs also fell inside Bath's city boundaries. These were the contents of two incendiary canisters, emptied out over the Odd Down area. The incendiary bombs contained thirty-six tubes, filled with powdered magnesium (a silvery-white metal which burns very brightly and was long used in flash-photography) to which a finned tail was attached. The tubes would be put into a specially designed basket and be dropped at the same time as normal bombs. The basket would float down on a parachute and part-way down spring-loaded gates would open allowing the incendiaries to fall out, igniting upon impact with a solid object, such as a roof. Unless they were extinguished quickly, by being covered for instance with sand or earth, they could cause major conflagrations. The resulting (minor) fires were swiftly extinguished and no loss of life was recorded. This was not the case with the next incident two months later.

On 16 March 1941, during Bristol's fifth heaviest air raid, two canisters of incendiaries and five high explosive bombs were dropped over Englishcombe Lane and Twerton, the latter area lying west of the centre and one of the city areas nearest Bristol. The incendiaries, which came down on Englishcombe Lane were dealt with quickly but the bombs in Twerton came down onto

The graves at Haycombe Cemetery of the three Randall children, killed when a stray bomb exploded in Twerton High Street, in March 1941.

buildings and not waste ground. These were two houses in Twerton High Street, one of which was empty, the other not. The occupied one was No.8 and six people – including three from the same family – lost their lives; twenty-six more were injured. Those killed were William Rogers, William Weston, Alexander Phillips, and three young members of the Randall family: Robert (12) Ellen (10) and Doris (6) all of whom had been evacuated from London to 'safe' Bath. A fourth sibling suffered fractured ribs and two broken arms. Two men who had been standing outside No.8 when it was hit were also killed, and another was killed from a bomb landing outside West Twerton School: according to a contemporary report, 'the man had come out of his house, turned and was hit by a piece of metal in his neck.'

Worse was to follow the next month, in both Bristol and Bath. The raid on 11 April 1941, Good Friday, on the bigger city, was devastating and merciless, and somewhere during the night, a lone German plane, most likely lost or returning home, dropped several 250-kilogramme high explosive bombs on the Dolemeads area of Widcombe in Bath: 'I was on my way to the control point at the bottom of Widcombe Hill when a plane came over,' stated eyewitness and police officer, Mr Jackson. 'I heard three bombs drop and saw a great sheet of flame go up. The bomb had hit the gas main.'

There were eleven fatalities, in Broadway, Excelsior Street and Princes Buildings. According to local blitz historian John Penny, 'Damage was also fairly widespread, and in addition to those who lost their lives, a further 52 men, women and children suffered various degrees of injury, all innocent victims of the so called "Good Friday" raid, Bristol's sixth and last, large scale attack.' Those killed in Bath included Mary Derrick, Elizabeth & William Gay, Georgina Lidgett, Robert Norris, Joe Dimery Seele, Patricia Sharman, Herbert Waterson, along with Geoffrey & Phoebe White.

It was said that over that Easter weekend the Prime Minister Winston Churchill was due to visit Bristol. On Good Friday his train passed through Bath but stopped for the night in a siding just west of Carr's Wood Tunnel near Twerton. That night Churchill was able to look out of his carriage window to see the glow of the fires to the west in Bristol, and also back towards Bath.

If the Battle of Britain was seen as a defiant gesture for the Allied cause, then what was perceived as its first actual victory, the routing of the enemy forces, came a few months later. Mussolini, intent on impressing not only his own people but Hitler, decided to undertake what he believed would be an easy task and invade neutral Greece. This had come about due to the Greek government's rejection of the Italian dictator's demand to station troops in their country. The famous 'No' (or *Ochi* in Greek) response by its prime minister is still celebrated – as Ochi Day – in Greece on 28 October each year. Hitler was not in favour of the plan but Mussolini invaded Greece anyway. As the Persians found to their cost many centuries earlier, the Greeks were no pushovers and at the end of 1940 and into early 1941 the Greek troops not only repelled the Italians from their own soil, but after doing so then pushed them far back into neighbouring Albania. An understandably furious Hitler, who had only recently lost his encounter with Britain's air-force, was now forced to act against Greece. This action consisted of a fully-fledged attack by the German 12th Army in April 1941 that resulted in the Swastika flying over the Acropolis several weeks later. The British government sent forces to Greece to help repel the invaders, unsuccessfully as it turned out, and inevitably Bath men were caught up in the fighting. On Sunday, 20 April, Second Lieutenant Arthur Roy Candy, from Bathampton, fighting with the Cyprus Regiment was killed. He was the son of Sidney and Mabel and is buried in the Phaleron War Cemetery, south-east of Athens, as is Robert Claude Cope, a 22-year-old LAC in the Air Force and son of Herbert and Dorothy Cope of Lambridge, who died later in this theatre of the war.

Four days later, Greece surrendered and the Greek army, its royal family and various Allied troops were evacuated to Crete, where they dug in to receive an anticipated sea-borne invasion. An invasion ensued, the only time in the annals of warfare a purely airborne invasion of an island had ever been undertaken. On 20 May 1941, German aircraft set off from airbases on the Greek mainland and an hour later the sky above Crete was filled with descending paratroopers. The fighting was intense, with many locals ferociously defending their home soil alongside Allied troops. But it was to no avail and ten days later the island fell to the invading German forces. While most Allied troops headed south towards the coast and possible evacuation to North Africa, the Cretans were left to brutal reprisals from the Germans. This was perhaps a taste of what might have befallen the British people, including the population of Bath, the previous year if the Battle of Britain had had a different outcome.

Deaths of other local men during this campaign included that of Edmund Pickett Ash, a 21-year-old private serving in the 308th Motor Transport Company of the Royal Army Service Corps. He died on Saturday, 26 April, and is remembered on the Athens Memorial.

While the Battle of Crete was still raging, on 22 May the Cruiser HMS *Gloucester* was sunk nearby by Axis aircraft. Of the more than 250 crew who perished, at least three were from Bath: 18-year-old Able Seaman Gerald Edward Dowding; Frederick James Hunt, a 21-year-old Stoker 1st Class; and 30-year-old Able Seaman Frederick William Smith. All three are commemorated on the Plymouth Naval Memorial.

CHAPTER 5

Songs, Sport & Strategies
(June 1941 – April 1942)

Back on the home front in June 1941, coupons were required to buy clothing, and the following month, coal was added to the ration. Despite these austere measures, the people of Bath tried to carry on with their daily life as normally as they could. Couples still married – many of the grooms being servicemen on leave – women still gave birth, and societies and groups around the city still organised outings and trips for their members not off fighting.

One example of the latter was the Bath Photographic Society. On Saturday, 7 June, they had an outing to St Catherine's Court where a meal (a 'repast') was taken, one of those present being Major Noel Harbutt, whose family was famous for the 'Plasticine' material made at their factory in Bathampton. The following Sunday, the 15th, the society held a joint outing with the Admiralty Camera Club to the Old Court Hotel near Avoncliffe.

Recycling: not a modern-day invention.

Above all, people wanted to be entertained; if anything, more so during this period, to take their minds off the war and the privations of almost every aspect of their daily lives. Other than outings and trips, there were several possibilities to escape from the realities of war, even if only for half an hour. Probably the most dominant single source of entertainment, certainly within households, was the wireless set. Not only was it the prime resource of news and information about the war, through the BBC Home Service, it was also the light entertainment service which broadcast such programmes as 'ITMA' (*It's That Man Again*), *Workers Playtime*, *Children's Hour*, and the Forces Programme; the latter being a twelve-hour daily entertainment dose for the troops that had begun back in 1940. Then of course there were Germany's English language radio transmissions that most (in)famously broadcast the propaganda of William Joyce, otherwise known as 'Lord Haw-Haw'. Although his broadcasts were meant to undermine the British people's confidence and lower their morale, the audience he attracted in Britain, for the most part, laughed at his words rather than become demoralised by them.

Magazines and newspapers were sources of entertainment, although as the war carried on and paper resources became scarce, this became a limited option. Nevertheless, the local newspaper, the *Bath and Wiltshire Chronicle and Herald*, was published throughout the war each weekday afternoon at 3 o'clock, price 1d, with a weekly edition being produced on Saturdays.

Another very popular show on the wireless was *Music While You Work*. The role music played in keeping morale high in the war is underestimated and there is no doubting that such songs as *We'll Meet Again* and *The White Cliffs of Dover*, both made famous by Vera Lynn, along with Flanagan & Allen's *Run Rabbit Run* and *(We're Gonna Hang Out) the Washing on the Siegfried Line* played their own important part in the war effort and ultimately victory over the enemy. This was down to the impact the recorded versions of the songs had through being played continuously on wireless sets, but also to the comradeship of people getting together around a pub piano on a Saturday night and singing them.

If the thought of a pub sing-a-long was not your cup of tea, there were several other options open to the people of Bath in wartime. One of these was the cinema. At the start of the war there was a nationwide government closure of cinemas, including those in Bath – the fear being that large numbers of people gathered together under one roof might lead to massive loss of life from the expected bombing raids. They soon reopened though, when these attacks failed to materialize. This was no doubt a huge relief to all those who would during the war years buy between 25 and 30 million tickets a week as they sought out the latest films that would allow them to escape from the realities of their own lives for a few hours. In Bath 'people queued for hours to see the latest films screened at the Beau Nash in Westgate Street, the Odeon and the Forum in Southgate, the Little Theatre in St Michael's Place, and the Scala at Oldfield Park.' Patriotic and romantic films such as *In Which We Serve* and *Casablanca* mixed with Hollywood epics such as *Gone with the Wind* and comedies like *Champagne Charlie is in Town* starring Tommy Trinder and Stanley Holloway, and George Formby's *He Snoops to Conquer*. During June 1941, cinema goers to the Forum in Southgate could watch Arthur Askey and Richard Murdoch in *The Ghost Train* – the film version of the play written by Bath's own Arnold Ridley.

If instead of mere celluloid adaptations, you preferred the real thing, Bath theatre-goers were more than amply catered for. The city had two theatres at the time, dramatically facing each other across the Sawclose. The Theatre Royal, which is still going strong today, moved to its present site in 1806, having previously been situated in Orchard Street, while the Palace Theatre, now sadly gone, stood opposite. Concerts also proved popular throughout the war years in Bath, and along with internationally famous performers and orchestras who visited the city to entertain audiences, there were also more permanent fixtures. These included Bath Philharmonic – directed by A. Ernest Monk – and the Pump Room Orchestra who, as their title would suggest, entertained visitors partaking of the spa waters, as the musicians of the ensemble had done for many centuries.

If a more physical experience was what was required from your musical evening, then the Pavilion, among other venues, catered for this through the numerous dances they ran. The Pavilion would also have more traditional programmes, such as in 1944 when the City of Birmingham Orchestra gave a concert, which included Grieg's Piano Concerto featuring Moura Lympany as the soloist, and the following year Solomon gave a recital there. To say farewell to 1941, the Assembly Rooms held its annual New Year's Eve Ball (although those present did not realise it at the time, this would be the last for a number of years).

If you wanted to watch physical exertion rather than partake of it yourself, you could stand on the terraces or touch-lines of the various sporting venues across the city. Although like cinema, sport had been initially banned at the outbreak of war – for the same reason of large crowds congregating in one place – this was also short-lived and sporting events returned to the city on a scale which, if not exactly equalling pre-war standards, still managed to bring enjoyment to countless spectators through the war years.

Football remained healthy in levels of playing standards, as pre-war professional footballers who were now serving in the forces and were stationed in the local military camps sought fixtures with the city's main club, Bath City FC. Some legendary names who played during this period included Stan Mortensen of

Blackpool and England fame, Chelsea's Vic Woodley and Johnny Jackson, the Wales international Sid Low, Bill Shankly (later to achieve football immortality as the Liverpool manager) and Dave McCulloch, who played for Derby County, as well as representing Scotland. Bath City FC, managed by Arthur Mortimer, won the wartime League Cup and their home games were often watched by crowds of more than 10,000 people; an FA Cup qualifying game against Aston Villa – which ended three all but saw Bath sadly lose the reply at Villa Park – attracted a gate of 17,000.

Like its sporting counterpart, Rugby also benefited from the establishment of military bases in the vicinity. Essential workers had come to the city from elsewhere – such as the Admiralty – and so for the crowds who gathered to watch their home side, there was always a sense of anticipation as to who was going to appear on the pitch, on either side. For example, the Bath side could boast three international caps in its line-up when the club met an RAF XV on the Recreation Ground in early 1942, these 'caps' being Gerrard, Shebean and D. Evans, who at international level represented England, Ireland and Wales.

To greater or lesser degrees, this situation existed through most other sports either played or watched in the city, although with certain ones, such as cricket, this encompassed county level as well. Cricket also, along with such sports as bowling, had to contend with many of their buildings, halls, pitches or greens being requisitioned for wartime purposes by such organisations as the Home Guard or ARP.

Horse racing had its ups and downs during the war. A two-day race meeting in August 1939 had been the final peacetime event before, like many other activities, it was banned. Fixtures recommenced once the 'Phoney War' got underway, although meetings could be cancelled at short notice. Even though Churchill gave orders for racing to be suspended from 10 May – the day the Germans invaded Western Europe – the Home Office gave permission for it to resume a week later. This meant the race meeting at the end of the month could take place, but any excitement felt over winners was overshadowed by the news coming from Dunkirk and many of the soldiers from the beaches were brought to the racecourse – the army having requisitioned part of the land – before being deployed elsewhere. This was the last race meeting during the war and no more would take place until April 1946, almost a year after victory in Europe, as major repairs and rebuilding had to be undertaken after six years of use by the War Office and, later, the Air Ministry as well.

By war's end, most sports in the city could no doubt compile a list of players who had lost their lives in the defence of their country, as well as those whose actions had resulted in official accolades and awards. Bath RFC was rightly proud that a former forward – Major Peter Morley – had been awarded the Military Cross, although mourned the news that several other players, including Captain Peter Moon and Lance Corporal Leslie Philips were now dead. Moon, a former Bath (and Somerset) forward as well as Lansdown cricketer, was killed in February 1944 while serving with the 8th Army in Italy. Lance Corporal Phillips of the 7th Battalion Parachute Regiment, a former star player, died in Normandy on D-Day.

Through the rest of 1941 and into 1942 the *Bath Chronicle* continued to report the sad deaths of other local men.

During June and July 1941, the 1st Cavalry Division, which included the North Somerset Yeomanry, took part in operations in Syria against the Vichy French. Amongst the casualties were two men from Bath, Troopers Lionel 'Bertie' Bryant and Douglas Mitchell. Bryant is buried in the Allied War Cemetery in Damascus.

The following month, a warship named after the city became another casualty of German U-boats. HNoMS *Bath* had begun life as USS *Hopewell,* a Wickes-class destroyer in the United States Navy. She was transferred to the British Royal Navy in September 1940 under the 'Destroyers for Bases' agreement whereby Britain received desperately needed ships in exchange for America's access to military bases in the Bahamas and elsewhere. On crossing the Atlantic, USS *Hopewell* was renamed HMS *Bath*, as part of the RN's Town-class destroyer series, which also included HMS *Salisbury, Brighton* and *Wells.* The 1,020-ton warship then underwent refit at HM Dockyard Devonport before being deployed to 1st Minelaying Squadron at Kyle of Lochalsh in Scotland. Once there, its duties included escorting convoys and minesweeping operations with the squadron. Another refit, in early 1941, saw the ship at Chatham dockyard, and on completion, in April that year, the vessel was transferred to the Royal Norwegian Navy and became HNoMS *Bath.* Operations as part of the 'Liverpool Escort Force' followed, which consisted of escorting convoys between the UK and Gibraltar. This part of its 'career' proved to be short-lived though, as on 19 August 1941, HNoMS *Bath* was sunk. The destroyer had left Liverpool on the 13th of the month as part of the escort for Convoy OG 71 (OG = Outbound, Gibraltar.) The convoy had reached a position about 350 miles south-west of Ireland when it was attacked by *U-204.* Hit by two torpedoes and breaking in half, HNoMS *Bath* sank in three minutes. Out of a crew of 128 there were 40 survivors, although no evidence has been found to suggest any men from the city the ship was named after were actually on board at the time of her demise.

In November, Operation Crusader began in the North African desert. The 7th Indian Infantry Brigade was part of 4th Indian Division and was tasked with capturing a position called Sidi Omar. During the sustained attack at least two

Bath men died. The first was killed in action on the 22nd. This was 26-year-old Alfred Nelson Blackmore, a lance corporal in the 1st Battalion the Royal Sussex Regiment. He is buried in Halfaya Sollum War Cemetery and is commemorated in the parish church at Swainswick. The 7th Indian Infantry Brigade was supported by the 42nd Royal Tank Regiment and one of their fatalities was 37-year-old Warrant Officer John Davies from Odd Down in Bath. He also lies in Halfaya Sollum Cemetery which lies at the foot of Halfaya or 'Hellfire' Pass, through the escarpment that separates the coastal plain from the inland plateau. The cemetery contains the remains of 2,046 men, 238 of whom are unidentified. Both men were married.

A few days later, on 27 November 1941, Lance Corporal Sidney John Elliott of the 1st Battalion of the Somerset Light Infantry died while serving with the Battalion in India. The 28-year-old was the son of William and Isabel of Bath and is buried in Rawalpindi War Cemetery.

In the final month of 1941, fatalities of local men included the names of Douglas Harold Greenwood, Norman Francis Durnell, Alfred George Bond, Herbert Alfred Archer, Alfred Samuel William Skelton, H. Commons and Peter Sheriff Charles. Apart from Royal Marine Corporal Greenwood and RAFVR Flight Lieutenant Charles, the rest were serving aboard a variety of ships when they died.

On Tuesday, 2 December 1941, the National Service Act was introduced. This meant that all single (or widowed) women between 20 and 30 years old (amounting to 1.7 million women) were now eligible to be called up, while the conscription age for men was expanded to between 18½ and 50.

The call-up of women was perhaps something of a double-edged sword, as the cause of women's emancipation which had witnessed such giant strides because of the First World War now gathered even more momentum during the second through this act. Not that the women of Bath needed the (male) government to pass a national act for them to do their bit for the war effort. In the 1914-18 conflict countless women were only too glad to volunteer in whatever capacity was required. As well as helping their men folk, carrying the war to Hitler on the frontlines, and the sense of independence they felt through earning their own money, must have had their own rewards. Nevertheless, the government's reliance on women volunteering had its limits, as one pair of authors recounted in their book on Bath's home front, and ultimately this led to the decision to include women in the next round of conscription:

> The shortage of manpower was becoming acute and special appeals were made by the mayor for women volunteers to serve in a long list of

non-combatant organisations that included the ARP, Auxiliary Fire Service, Civil Nursing Reserve, British Red Cross Society, WVS, Women's Land Army, Blood Transfusion Service, the Army and LDV. In June 1941, Bath's Ministry of Information Committee held a big recruitment drive to encourage women to join the forces and war factories and backed it up with a huge parade of women's services.

Once conscription was introduced, the *Bath Chronicle* was able to announce its estimation that between 600 and 700 women in the city had registered for National Service on the first Saturday after its introduction. The recruitment of women for the armed forces and war work continued throughout the war, with the campaign being kept alive locally by photographs and articles in the *Bath Chronicle* showing Bath women 'doing a fine job for the war effort'.

As in the previous world war, many women would find themselves in roles normally associated with men, such as porters at the GWR goods station. Roles more traditionally female-orientated were no less important though. These included caring for soldiers convalescing in local hospitals – through the Co-operative Women's Guild – and Civil Defence fire watchers through the Women's Volunteer Service. Members of the WVS became active in demonstrating schemes for setting up house in 48 hours following an air raid. Other non-compulsory roles saw women volunteers packing food parcels and small gifts for the armed forces at Christmas, most of the wrapping taking place at local church halls, while housewives were encouraged to set up street savings groups.

For many women, some of these roles, although important in attaining victory, were not viewed as gaining any real power or advancement for the cause of women in general. On the other hand, of the five newly appointed magistrates for the city in 1942, two were women: Mrs Robert Pitt and Miss Kathleen Harper.

On 7 December 1941, the Japanese attacked Pearl Harbor and brought America into the war. Simultaneously, they began their Malayan campaign, which would ultimately result in the fall of Singapore, Britain's major military base in the Far East. Two days into this campaign, tragedy struck when HMS *Repulse* and *Prince of Wales* were sunk. Both battleships had a Bath man on board. On the former was Norman Francis Durnell, a 19-year-old able seaman and son of Frederick and Gertrude of Bath. He is commemorated on the Plymouth Naval Memorial. Meanwhile, Alfred George Bond was on HMS *Prince of Wales*. He was 36 and the foster son of Mrs A. Barnett of Bath. Like Durnell, he was an able seaman RN and his name is on the Plymouth Memorial.

On Wednesday, 21 January 1942, during the Malayan campaign, Richard John French, a 20-year-old 2nd Lieutenant in the 5/18th Battalion of the Garhwal Rifles, was killed. The Garhwals were part of the 45th Indian Infantry Brigade. After the war, Kranji War Cemetery was opened in the north of Singapore island containing the remains of 3,702 men; 2nd Lieutenant French was amongst them. Within Kranji War Cemetery is the Singapore Memorial to those who died during the Malaya campaign and elsewhere, and who have no known grave. It was unveiled on 2 March 1957 by the then Governor of Singapore, Sir Robert Black, and has 24,317 names inscribed upon it.

William Henry Shellard was a 20-year-old Gunner in the 6th Heavy Anti-Aircraft Regiment, RA. He was in the 12th Battery of the regiment when he died on 1 March 1942. He was the son of Thomas and Sophia of South Stoke and is remembered on the Rangoon Memorial.

After the surrender of Singapore, on Sunday, 15 February 1942, large numbers of people – as individuals or in groups – tried to escape to safety. One such group was on the ship HMS *Anking*. One of the crew was Chief Petty Officer (Cook) Frederick William Price, from Bath. The ship had reached some 200 miles east of Christmas Island when she was attacked by Japanese warships and sunk. Price was amongst those who died in the attack, on Wednesday, 4 March 1942.

In February 1942, in the aftermath of Hitler's decision to transfer most of his aircraft to the east, RAF Bomber Command was informed by the Air Ministry, 'It has been decided that the primary objective of your operations should now be focussed on the morale of the enemy civil population, and in particular of the industrial workers.' This change of emphasis was put into action near the end of March 1942, when the Baltic port of Lübeck, and then not long after, Rostock, were heavily bombed. Instead of concentrating on the harbour and industrial areas, the cities' medieval and historic centres were targeted, most of which were destroyed. So incensed was the German leader about this wanton destruction that in the middle of April he signed order number 55672/42, which instructed the Luftwaffe's High Command, 'When targets are being selected, preference is to be given to those where attacks are likely to have the greatest possible effect on civilian life. Besides raids on ports and industry, terror attacks of a retaliatory nature are to be carried out against towns other than London.' The first results of this directive came on the night of 23 April 1942 when Exeter became the target for German bombers stationed in northern France. The following night it was attacked again.

A few days earlier, on Monday, 20 April 1942, a regional team of five senior inspectors – known as the 'Circus' and headed by Chief Regional Inspector Speare – descended on Bath to inspect its firebomb defences. The visit was arranged, according to the minutes of the Fire Prevention Conference which took place the following day, between the high-powered team and local representatives, as the city 'met with their objective to inspect the most important towns in the region' and stated as its purpose: 'In order to see exactly what is the state of the present development and to give instruction and advice for its improvement and extension'. During the conference, its chairman, Major Lock, assured Mr Speare and his associates that all aspects of the city's firebomb defences were more than adequately covered, and the organisation of the Fire Guard was now under his supervision. In addition, according to George Scott in his thought-provoking essay *Firebomb Fiasco*, Lock produced a 'promissory note signed up to by great and good organisations of Bath'. This document stated that the major had 'appointed a Fire Prevention Advisory Committee to deal with the various Fire Prevention matters including representatives of the Admiralty, Chamber of Commerce, Trades Union Council and Education Authority.'

Like the council's announcement back in September 1939 – 'In the absence of an actual attack to test the effectiveness of the machinery, everything possible has been done to ensure the safety of our population in an emergency' – Major Lock's assurance and documentation at this conference were still mere words until put to the ultimate test of an 'actual attack'. Unknown to everyone at the table, this ultimate test would come less than a week later.

CHAPTER 6

Fire of Annihilation (April 1942)

The Second World War lasted nearly six years and during this period many events occurred to change the city of Bath, as well as the people living within it. But everything else that happened seems to pale into insignificance when compared to the events of one weekend in late April 1942.

Saturday, 25 April 1942, had been a sunny and bright spring day and the forecast was for a clear, moonlit night. The weekly edition of the *Bath Chronicle* had been published as usual and its front page mixed news from the war with more localised stories. Several of the war reports were centred on men from the city missing in action, such as Chief Petty Officer Harold (Peter) Herman, RN, of 2 Ringwood Road, Oldfield Park, who had survived the sinking of HMS *Repulse* back in early December 1941 but had now been heard of in Singapore two days before Christmas.

On the 'home front', the newspaper reported a suggestion to the Bath Parks Committee to use the Sydney Gardens band lawn for a weekly dance throughout the summer. Having given 'sympathetic consideration to the application', it was noted, 'the Committee left the settlement of arrangements in the hands of the Chairman.' Directly beneath this story was another one of local interest. Topped by the headline 'Bath Fire Guard Officer Resigns', this smallish, twenty-four-line article reported the official announcement – made at a meeting of the Bath Civil Defence Committee the day before – of Mr C.S. Welch's voluntary departure as Fire Guard Staff Officer for Bath. According to the report, Mr Welch had been confronted with difficulties in obtaining a house in, or near, Bath and so this had made the carrying out of his duties much harder. In addition, family illnesses had increased his anxieties, and this had no doubt been a contributing factor to his own recent poor state of health. Welch would be on leave until the end of that month, at which time his connection with Civil Defence work in Bath would be severed. In the meantime, Welch's deputy, Mr R.W.J. Gardner, would continue to assume, as acting staff officer, the responsibilities of his former boss.

If events had transpired differently, this minor news story, which reading between the lines was a prime example of the 'gardening leave' scenario, would have remained a negligible piece of information on a yellowing cutting archived in a dust-covered box somewhere. Obviously of significance to the city's now ex-fire officer, this was probably of much less importance to the rest of Bath's population than the possibility of a new weekly dance in beautiful surroundings over the coming months.

The city's population would remain unaware of it, but this news item's relevance to them would be greatly amplified several hours later, at one minute to eleven at night to be precise, when the first air-raid siren that evening sounded. And while the events leading up to C.S. Welch's resignation and the consequences arising from it might seem insignificant in themselves, when put within the context of the city's overall civil defence organisation, the ramifications were massive.

During that Saturday evening, an air armada comprising around eighty German planes from various units took off from airfields in northern France. After crossing the Channel, the first wave of bombers reached the English coast at 10.25 pm over Bridport, and then headed north towards their intended target for that night: Bath. On board one of the aircraft was Gunther Hoenicke, a German war reporter given the rank of *Sonderführer*, whose account of that night's bombing would appear the following day in the Nazis' own newspaper under the headline: Bath – Fire of Annihilation:

> On the British coast the first searchlights flashed up. The Tommies don't yet know where the bombers are heading; they think they are well protected in Bath.

For most in Bath, the air-raid siren that began wailing at 10.59 pm on that Saturday night was the signal for another probable attack on neighbouring Bristol, which had been a regular target for the German bombers since June 1940. Those in the aircraft fast approaching the city, however, knew differently. Exeter had been the first to feel the effects of Hitler's 'retaliatory' attacks on the previous two evenings, but tonight, as the inhabitants of the city was about to discover, it was Bath's turn.

> Beneath, the River Avon winds through the country like a silver thread. Here below us is the great loop in the middle of which lies the town, and now too the first small incendiaries go down.

Despite the blackout, which had officially begun seven minutes before the air-raid siren had sounded, visibility around the moonlit city was near perfect. This meant that those people on higher ground – either carrying out their civic duties, such as fire-watching, or else perhaps returning from a night out – could see with terrifying clarity German aircraft approaching on the horizon and then watch, with increasing understanding of the reality, the first incendiary devices fall, thus announcing Bath as the Germans' main target for that night.

German bombers normally flew in groups of three and, as far as the research for this book shows, compiled from printed sources, contemporary reports and eye-witness accounts, the first group – three Junkers 88s – came in low over the surrounding hills from the north-east, around a quarter-of-an-hour after the siren sounded. The city, bathed in light from a 'bombers' moon', was completely vulnerable as it lay stretched out in front of the German aircrews readying themselves to offload their deadly cargo.

This night of terror will go down in Bath's history.

The middle aircraft of the group dropped its load – four bombs and a basket of incendiaries – roughly along the line of St Saviours Road, in the Larkhall area of the city. The first bomb fell somewhere near Ferndale Road, the second near Spa Lane Bridge, the third in the road between Lambridge Lodge and Elmcroft, demolishing a wall and bursting the water main, and the fourth hit 18 Beaufort West (now Worcester Cottage) and finished up in the road without exploding. The incendiaries meanwhile fell mostly over Brooklyn Road, near to where the second bomb had fallen. It is still possible today to observe the wall between Lambridge Lodge and Elmcroft and see where it was rebuilt afterwards.

The left-hand aircraft of this first group released its bombs a moment later, with one of them making a direct hit on the 'Grosvenor Brewery', a public house near Grosvenor Bridge, also known as 'The Folly', not far from the Lambridge area. The building was destroyed, although some of the remains, including the entrance steps, can still be seen. A few of the incendiaries from this bomber fell into the nearby Kennet and Avon canal, to cause a considerable bomb-scare many years later.

The remaining Junkers 88 of the group – flying in the 'right-hand' position – dropped its bombs on the Fairfield Park area with one of them detonating just behind the Fairfield Arms public house. It seems more than likely that a bomb from this stick also demolished five houses in Hanover Terrace.

We roar down from the sky, now the first flares from our leaders light up the land like day!

The main German force – comprising mainly Dorniers Do 217s and Junkers 88s accompanied by older Heinkel 111s and Dorniers Do 17s – arrived above the city and began attacking closer to the centre. If there was complacency

Hanover Terrace in Bath, then and now.

regarding the Germans' target for that night initially, it was swiftly dispelled. 'I was at the top of the steps,' one eyewitness standing in his Twerton garden later recalled, 'when I saw the first chandelier [string of flares] across the south-east slopes of the city, over Southdown. I said, "Bath is for it."'

Along with these pathfinder flares, dropped to illuminate the city for the rapidly approaching bombers (although the moon was already doing an efficient job of that), thousands of incendiary bombs and several tons of high-explosive bombs would also be dropped on the city during this first raid. An early bomb hit one of the gas holders located on the Upper Bristol Road (possibly the one which had the word 'Bath' scrubbed off before the war as a precautionary measure to hide the identity of the city from the enemy) and the results were spectacular for those viewing from above:

Suddenly, in front of us a great towering flame appears which dazzles us with its flaming red, even in the cockpit! . . . A gas-holder has exploded in the gas works. In a second the fire spreads and casts a flaming light over the city.' . . . Our commander calmly searches for a new target.

*Stothert & Pitt's
Newark works
was heavily
damaged during
the Bath Blitz.*

Bombs now fell indiscriminately, mainly in the Upper Bristol Road and Kingsmead areas, destroying numerous houses and killing many of their inhabitants who had chosen to stay put rather than seek out the nearest shelter. It was in this latter area that one of the worst tragedies of this raid occurred. A trio of bombs came to ground almost simultaneously, causing extensive damage to the surroundings. The initial pair landed in Kingsmead Square, while the third fell a little further west in New King Street. A large crater was created as the high-explosive bomb burst in the road, shattering windows and demolishing two large Georgian terraced houses in the adjacent street as they fell in on themselves; some took this to indicate that these buildings had been poorly constructed. One of the houses was No.7 New King Street. It was occupied, and eleven people died, including seven members of the Ford family – six children and their mother. With more deaths in other houses in the immediate vicinity, the death toll attributed to just this one bomb ultimately totalled twenty.

The perhaps poor construction of the Georgian houses was counteracted by the large cellars they put below and which, in many cases, extended out underneath the road, saving the lives of many who chose to shelter in them. Above ground, although several houses did completely collapse, including those in New King Street, countless other people owed their lives to the fact their homes, and particularly stairwells, stood up surprisingly well to the German bombardment. A problem that quickly arose, however, was the amount of dust that Bath Stone produced when caught in a blast. Not only could it cause respiratory problems, but also infections if it came into contact with open wounds.

Above: New King Street after the first raid; twenty people were killed by this bomb.

Below: The Ford family graves, consisting of Mrs Ford and six of her children.

More bombers approach and again and again there are explosions as one wave after another passes over the town, bringing death and destruction.

As well as the gas holder receiving a direct hit, a gas main near Crescent Gardens had been severed. It burned through the night and the bomb that caused it brought down nearby houses and cut the telephone link to the Civil Defence Centre based at Apsley House. From then on, it had to rely on messengers to communicate with staff spread out across the city. Elsewhere, the fire service sub-station at Modern Motors had to be abandoned, after boiling creosote spewed out from the damaged gas holder. Marlborough Lane and Holloway were deliberately bombed, while a solitary stray high-explosive bomb landed on the Recreation Ground, turning its west stand into a pile of twisted metal. Other bombs hit the historic Abbey Church House – shattering its east window – and the LMS Railway Goods Yard. At least one bomb exploded in St James's cemetery, opposite the yard, violently throwing plumes of earth into the air and disturbing long-dead corpses from their eternal rest. Present-day residents, the Cuttings, lived in Kingsmead Terrace. After their house took a direct hit from a bomb, which killed four of the family – Amelia, John, Norah and Terence – the surviving members remained trapped until Monday before they were dug out after another relative came to check on them.

A black cloud of smoke hangs over the city

When the 'all clear' finally sounded at 1.20 in the morning, the 'death and destruction' which had been brought from the air consisted of eighty-eight people dead and numerous buildings damaged or completely wrecked. Among the dead were civilians, who had been killed in their houses, and members of the various civil defence organisations – Home Guard, ARP wardens, fire-fighters – who had been killed while carrying out their duties. Not only were they victims of bomb blasts, but also of the machine-gun fire from German gunners, intent on stopping them doing their duty.

The people of Bath were in total shock. The city had not been considered a risk and so there had been no anti-aircraft defences around the perimeter. Now the task of rescuing people from damaged and collapsed buildings, tending to the injured and clearing up the unholy wreckage could begin in earnest. Meanwhile, the authorities, according to the *Bath Chronicle,* 'were trying to take stock of the situation. Casualties and the homeless were brought to rest centres, while the fire services [many of whom had earlier headed off to Bristol before realising it was in fact Bath that was tonight's target] struggled to put out the blazes that had

*The North Stand
on the Recreation
Ground.*

*Like St Paul's in
London, Bath Abbey
rises defiantly through
the ruins.*

started in many buildings. Householders whose property had been less seriously damaged started to clear up the mess.'

And then, inexplicably, unbelievably and terrifyingly, less than three hours after the all-clear had sounded, the siren began to wail again, at around four o'clock in the morning and another wave of aircraft could be heard in the distance. These were many of the same aircraft from the first raid who had by now returned to their airfields in France and, having refuelled and replenished their bomb bays, made a second journey back across the channel.

The second raid, by now the early hours of Sunday, wreaked havoc. Even though there were fewer aircraft this time around, more people died, and more buildings were wrecked than in the first raid. Oldfield Park bore the brunt of this attack and most of the 140 or so people who were killed lost their lives in this area. There were direct hits or explosions in Roseberry Road, King Edward Road,

Oldfield Park was one of the areas that suffered most from the air raids.

Thornbank Place, Elm Grove Terrace and Cheltenham Street, among others, as well as substantial damage inflicted on the recently completed St Bartholomew's Church. Several explosions rocked Moorland Road – the main shopping thoroughfare of Oldfield Park – and the Livingstone pub was set ablaze. The most tragic event of this raid was probably the direct hit that landed on the air-raid shelter outside the Scala Cinema. According to Niall Rothnie, the shelter was 'of a more substantial type than the ordinary street ones. It was semi-sunk tubular steel shelter, surrounded by earth and sand bags.' Ultimately though, it was little defence against the bomb which fell on it and caused multiple casualties. It has never been established how many people died in this blast, but it is known that eight special constables and at least six civilians perished. Most of the victims came from Third Avenue. For one of the special constables – C.W. Parsons – it was to be his first and last day on duty. However, as the bomb only hit one end of the shelter there were survivors, and these included the family who had returned from having a cup of tea at home between the raids. Finding their former places had been taken at the end of the shelter that would be hit, they were forced to go the other end of the shelter; thus their lives were saved.

Twerton also received heavy bombing and the Kingsmead area, already ablaze from the first raid, suffered further damage. Elsewhere, Apsley House, the Civil Defence HQ, having had its communications cut in the initial raid, now suffered a near miss which put the centre out of action completely.

Graves of the Rattray family; killed in the second raid of the Bath Blitz.

Many of the Somerset 5th (Bath City) Battalion Home Guard had been out and about helping where they could and inevitably some paid the ultimate price. One of the bodies recovered was that of Private Coles. Phillip 'Phil' Francis George Coles was the 20-year-old son of Charles Thomas and Caroline Annie Coles. They lived at Cottle's Buildings, Upper Weston (next to the Crown and Anchor). He had been deemed unfit to go into the regular army and so joined the Home Guard. He was on guard duty along the Upper Bristol Road when a bomb fell and brought a building down on top of him. Phil Coles was privately buried in Locksbrook Cemetery, but he has a War Graves Commission headstone. He was one of the eight members of this home guard battalion to be killed in the raids.

At about 5.30 on the Sunday morning, the all-clear sounded. As dawn broke the citizens of Bath left their places of shelter to survey a scene of utter devastation. With the return of daylight some went back to their homes, if they were still there, and got on with their lives. Many young lads cycled off to see what could be seen and to try to collect souvenirs. The city presented an incredible sight. Kingsmead Street was cordoned off and people looking down it from behind the barricades could see heaps of rubble and groups of workmen desperately trying to find and rescue any survivors.

As the day wore on, the sky became overcast, with a strengthening easterly wind. In anticipation of another possible raid, large swathes of people deserted built-up areas on the Sunday night to seek shelter in the nearby hills and countryside surrounding the city. One 12-year-old was taken by his mother to the section of Solsbury Lane where it descends into Batheaston. Several hundred yards of the lane were sunk to a depth of eight to ten feet, forming a wide trench. On arriving there, they found it already had people lying down trying to get some sleep. They found a space and settled down for the night. Other 'trekkers' on the other side of the city had a lucky escape. Having left Weston village and made their way up Lansdown Hill, they lay down on one side of a wall and went to sleep. During the night an anti-aircraft gun was set up the other side of it and, had it fired, no doubt the sleepers would have been caught in its blast.

With nightfall everyone who was not asleep was alert and waiting for something to happen. Sunday became Monday though, and all was quiet. Then at 1.15 am on the Monday morning the sirens went once more and for the next fifty minutes, until the all-clear sounded at 02.05 am, German aircraft circled the skies and, as before, dropped their bombs at will. Most bombs dropped during this raid were the one kg incendiary type, and nearly 8,000 of them made their way to earth, producing numerous fires which would ravage the city and gut many of its famous Georgian buildings.

The Bath Blitz is front page news.

The reasons behind the complete devastation caused by this raid are several-fold, although probably the main two are the fact that many buildings had had their roofs blown off in the previous raids and so their inflammable contents were like tinderboxes, ready to be ignited; and second, as well as the Fire Service being stretched beyond their capacity, there was a vast exodus of fireguards during this second night and so many of the fires, which should have been put out swiftly, were left to rage for hours, destroying everything in their paths. This is not to throw criticism at those men and women in the fire service and AFS, but the breakdown of leadership on this second night, leading to an absence of enough fire guards to deal with incendiary devices as they came to ground, can be traced back to a series of events stretching back to September 1939, with one of the most recent indications that this was a disaster waiting to happen coming with the newspaper report of C.S. Welch's resignation, which had been reported in the press only two days before.

Extensive damage was inflicted across the city. A near miss at St Martin's Hospital nevertheless wrecked X-ray equipment, while West Twerton School was badly damaged by another near miss. Fuller's Garage in Kingsmead Street caught fire and blew up, probably the result of a fuel tank exploding, while Holy Trinity Church was gutted by fire. Two more churches were destroyed

The damaged Francis Hotel, after the third raid...

Above: ...and the same scene, nearly eighty years on.

Below: Kingsmead Street was in another area heavily damaged by the raids. According to certain historians it was the epicentre of both nights' raids.

by fire: St Andrew's in Julian Road and St James's on the junction of Stall Street and Henry Street. The Kingsmead area received intense bombing for a third successive time; one reason for this, recounted by Rothnie in his book on the blitz, is that during the first night the German bombers had flown on a west-east axis, the second night north-south, and the paths of these had crossed directly over Kingsmead Square. In James Street West the newly built Labour Exchange was badly pitted by a near miss and then after incendiaries fell on the roof of the two-storey building the top floor was completely burnt down.

Further north in the city, the famous Assembly Rooms caught fire and were

What remained of the Regina Hotel.

mostly burned out – having only been reopened four years before. This fire was probably caused by the blast which destroyed one side of the nearby Regina Hotel. Thirty died in the Regina Hotel blast, most of the dead being guests who had declined to go down to the specially strengthened basement and had stayed in their rooms. The Francis Hotel, opposite Queen Square, also took a direct hit. There were only around five casualties here, as most of the guests had decided, unlike at the Regina, to head downstairs. Among the survivors were members of the Sadler's Wells orchestra, but their instruments, left in their rooms, were destroyed.

Most of the bombs dropped in the third raid were incendiary but there were also high-explosive ones again and several areas received large numbers of these. One area was south of the river – from Holloway and Beechen Cliff up to Bear Flat. It had suffered some damage on the first night, but this time it was worse. Almost all the roads in Poets Corner took direct hits. Shakespeare Avenue saw at least three dead – three women who had decided to stay home this evening, having gone to the public shelter the first night.

It wasn't only bombs that inflicted injuries and fatalities; machine-gun fire too, mainly aimed at hampering efforts to contain fires, accounted for a good many of the 146 people killed in this raid, as well as others in the previous ones. One of the victims was a lieutenant of the Gloucestershire Regiment, a detachment of which

THICK GREY DUST covered houses and roadway after the havoc caused in the Bath thoroughfare by Nazi raiders.

MANY FAMOUS BATH BUILDINGS WRECKED

Continued from Page 1

human and architectural. Working-class houses were reduced to rubble and whole families wiped out.

Historic houses and public buildings felt the effects of blast, but the fabric remains.

Much valuable stained glass was blown out of churches, and a number of suburban churches and chapels were partly demolished.

Several whole shopping centres were left with hardly a pane of glass intact, and goods were scattered over the streets.

But the people put on a brave face and the flag of St. George still floated above a church tower. In the afternoon a cinema opened.

shelters and riddling cars with bullet holes

One family of four was rescued from beneath the debris of a three-storey house with only one casualty—a scratched hand.

The local fire-fighting services were augmented from surrounding centres, and members of the W.V.S. drove their mobile canteens through streets lighted by blazing buildings and handed out hot drinks to firemen while the raid was still on.

Among the procession of people travelling to reception centres in various parts of the city carrying assortments of salved household goods were a number of London evacuees who were seeking sanctuary for the second time.

An officer of the N.F.S. on the spot told me that the fire-fight-

are all civilians. Women most of them.

Dawn broke over the drunkenly-tottering skeletons of what had been happy homes a few hours before.

A group of fire-watchers were talking quietly on a street corner.

"Two elderly women killed there . . . five up in that road . . . a woman and child . . . "

And in the distance a fire glowed . . .

That was the aftermath of an hour and a quarter raid which could not be interpreted as anything but an act of barbarous reprisals.

Several Killed

The local newspaper reveals the terrible news.

was stationed at St Mary Magdalene Church on Holloway. Around twenty-five men from the regiment had been sent by the army to assist in fire-watching duties and the church was being used as their temporary base. During the raid a warden was coming down Holloway when he passed three of the soldiers standing in the church porch opposite. The warden was 'on patrol coming down from the Bear Flat. You were always told to keep near the wall. I'd just said hello to the men, although

I didn't say anything about how dangerous it was, standing out there. It was very clear both nights and you could see the air gunners very low. I'd just got to the horse trough when I heard a burst of machine-gun fire. I dived for cover near the trough, in the road under the wall. I looked back. Two of the men were on the ground. One had his head shot off. The second was hit in the leg. The third wasn't hit at all.'

Another three members of the Somerset 5th (Bath City) Battalion Home Guard also died in this raid. One of them was Corporal W. Walsh, the other two were friends, Frederick James Park (17) and Allan Woods (19). They had been out during the first two raids, helping where they could, but during this one they were specifically on fire-watch at Norton Dairies in Circus Mews when the building took a direct hit and they were both killed. They are buried together at St Michael's Cemetery at Lower Weston.

By the time dawn broke on the Monday morning, there were thirty-five major fires burning across the city. A lost property office was set up at the Guildhall, but it was soon overwhelmed by the volume of items being brought in from the

The graves of Privates F.J. Park (17) and A.R. Woods (19) of the 5th Somerset (Bath City) Battalion Home Guard, killed on 26 April 1942 during the Bath Blitz; friends in life, side by side in eternal peace in death.

*The Dolemeads area of Bath suffered extensive damage before and during the Bath Blitz.
Apparently this image was censored at the time, in case it had a demoralising effect.*

various bomb sites. Large numbers of Bath men were serving overseas in the armed forces and, naturally, they were desperate to know if their families were alright. A special military enquiries office was set up in the Pump Room for this purpose, manned by four army officers.

On the Monday night, large numbers of people again trekked out into the countryside, but the Luftwaffe had moved on and that evening it was the people of Norwich who suffered at the hands of the German bombers; although the next day (Tuesday) a lone German plane flew over Bath photographing the damage.

The last survivor was pulled out from under the rubble at about nine o'clock in the evening on Wednesday, 29 April, although the bodies of the dead were still being recovered three months later. There were three mass funerals. The first was at Haycombe Cemetery on Friday, 1 May. A battalion of the Welsh Guards, billeted in the area at the time, dug the grave into which 247 people were interred. The next day, Saturday, the king and queen visited the city. They signed the official visitors book at the Guildhall and then spent an hour and a half touring the city. Another two funerals took place the following week. The official figure of those who died in the raids on Bath was 417, although this number did not appear until much later and even now this most likely falls short of the actual number who lost their lives during those two terrifying nights.

One of the mass graves at Haycombe Cemetery.

Afterwards the city was provided (somewhat belatedly) with anti-aircraft defences, including twelve two-inch rocket projectors, eight 40mm Bofors guns, and five German Flak guns. The batteries were placed under the officer commanding the Somerset 6th (Bath Admiralty) Battalion. As time would prove, they would not be required.

Left: The mass grave of blitz victims at Haycombe Cemetery.

Below: Map showing the location of the 'Blitz Graves'.

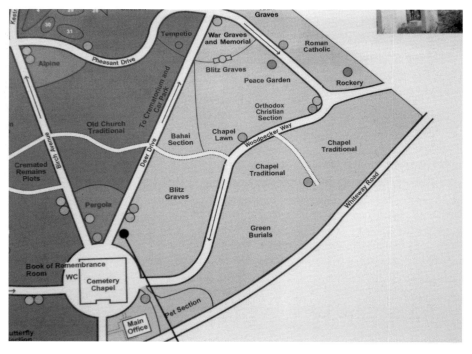

CHAPTER 7

Firebombs, Fire Guards & Failures (May 1942)

In his essay 'Firebomb Fiasco: Civil Defence in World War II', which first appeared in the anthology *Bath Exposed: Essays on the Social History of Bath, 1775-1945,* George Scott tells the story of the city's preparations, inadequacies and the various controversies that surrounded them, summing up with the damning conclusion that 'the raids of April 1942 exposed a significant gap in [Bath's] defence arrangements [and as] a result, a humiliating record of these deficiencies exists that ranks as one of the most ignominious accorded to any provincial city during the war.'

Even with the hindsight of only a few years, the official history of the Home Front, published by HMSO in 1950, was equally damning. 'Training was inadequate and equipment defective; in many buildings there were no fire guards

Lansdown Place East, where a chequered flag marks the spot of an unexploded bomb.

at all and a lack of leadership contributed to an exodus of fire guards on the second night.' The author, Terence H. O'Brien, revealed the origin of this 'brief and acerbic comment' as coming from *The Story of No. VII South Western Region*, published in 1946, and then went on to combine more statements from that publication along with his own observations: 'Early experience of fire watching in the region is generally characterised by: "Hesitant planning, of deference to public prejudice, of non-cooperation and even obstruction by local authorities and divided responsibilities," sentiments that echo much of what happened in Bath. The city is, however, singled out for special criticism of a nature that doubtless reflected the deep displeasure the event really meant to the Regional Commissioner, General Sir Hugh Elles.'

Probably most damning of all was the fact that while the 'circus' was still in town, so to speak, Major Lock's assurance of adequate preparations was thoroughly undermined by the man who had stepped into C.S. Welch's shoes after his resignation. This is not an attempt to 'witch-hunt' individuals – most in positions of responsibility acted honourably and rose to the challenge the raids and their aftermath produced. But rather, as Scott suggests, 'by reconstructing the relationship between pre-raid civic decision-making and its failure to sustain the adaptive behaviour required to cover the firebomb risk, a sharper perception of the events that gave rise to this indictment can be attained.'

Undoubtedly many in Bath were complacent until the first flares came floating down on that Saturday night, but not all, as a letter to the *Bath Chronicle* a few weeks before the raid indicates:

> Like many others I am wondering what will happen to the residential part of our City if we get an incendiary bomb raid. The complacency of many of the residents is remarkable. In my own particular district, as far as I know, we have no organiser; no roster of duties and no one takes very much interest in the possibility of such an event . . . Have we forgotten what happened at Bristol last Good Friday?

Although conjecture, part of this lack of urgency may have been due to the fact that the government did not believe Bath would be attacked or, if they believed or knew otherwise, did nothing about it. The reason given by the 1946 publication was, 'Bath... had been considered a safe town and perhaps for that reason was found virtually unprepared.' In the summer of 1939, the city was categorised as a 'reception' area. Bristol on the other hand, just down the road, was evacuating its population. But by the end of that year, Bath's safe label was no longer valid. Now the area was surrounded by many of the most secret and important locations in the country. The industrial area on the Lower Bristol Road housed Stothert & Pitt's Newark and Victoria Works, Horstmann Gear Company's Albion Works, and other factories that became engaged in war work. With the coming of the Admiralty and the secret work it was involved in – without the Mulberry Harbour, designed in Bath, there could have been no successful D-Day landings and therefore no victory against Hitler – it is complete nonsense to believe the government had not raised the status of the city to something other than 'safe'. It is possible that the government did realise the increased importance Bath but that by putting up defences it would draw attention to the city – just as putting huge padlocks on a gate might indicate to potential thieves that there is something of value inside.

Bath's Stothert & Pitt built these human torpedoes.

The company's headquarters after the raid.

There is the question of how much the Germans really knew about Bath's importance. Although the raids would become part of wartime folklore as 'Baedeker Raids', the reality is that when the bombers did arrive, both the Royal Crescent and the Circus, probably the two most iconic buildings of Bath, although suffering some damage, were for the most part left intact, while the industrial heartland, where vital work towards the war effort took place and the residential areas where many of its workers lived, were devastated. Given the visibility and the freedom the aircrews enjoyed while over the city, it seems that if cultural revenge was the reason for their visit, then not a brick would have been left standing of the moon-shaped crescent or sun-shaped circus. The shock of losing both these monuments might, to the people of Bath and indeed the whole world, have been in the same category as the seismic effect of the destruction of the twin towers in New York.

Although both suffered some damage, the 'twin towers' of Bath remained virtually unscathed after the raids.

Whatever any reasoning behind the decision not to protect Bath, the loss of life and damage to the city's buildings could have been lessened if adequate anti-aircraft and firebomb defences had been in place. Fewer roofless buildings would have been exposed on the second night, and the devastation of the second night, if it indeed it had happened at all, would have been dramatically decreased and who knows how many lives would have been saved.

To understand what went wrong in Bath, there are two main aspects to consider – the local and the national. The difference between how the government officially viewed and how it *truly* viewed Bath in terms of potential risk, we may never know. In terms of the local though, it is probably best seen through the story of fire watching in the city. Fire-watching regulations in the early part of the war were over-complicated and gave rise to confusion, resentment and ridicule. Compulsory fire-watching should have been introduced sooner and the process of exemption simplified. That the Fire Guard organisation became bogged down in the huge backlog of forms for exemption when its members should have been out recruiting instead, perhaps lies at the heart of the matter. One of the key events surrounding this issue remains the one regarding compulsory fire-watching. Frank Robinson, who had been employed to assemble the disparate set of legal and moral obligations that existed at the time of his appointment into a unified system of protection, became increasingly frustrated at what he saw as a lack of cooperation in regard to his request that fire-watching become compulsory. On 21 May 1941, a meeting of Bath's Emergency Committee decided to defer a decision about introducing compulsory Fire Guard and this happened again on 9 June.

By July 1941, Bath Fire Watch looked impressive, at least on paper. Robinson reported that there were 24,000 voluntary fire-watchers in the area. It appears, however, that to achieve these numbers the training had been somewhat scant.

It also seems that different sets of regulations for residential and commercial premises caused problems. Naturally, employers who were required to provide their own watch ordered their staff to give precedence to the Fire Watch over any other commitments they might have, such as the Home Guard. The scheme for residential property was voluntary, so where commercial and residential properties were in the same block, as they often were, many householders did not see why they should put their lives at risk during an air raid when the business next door would protect their property for them. Another bone of contention was that some firms employed paid fire-watchers.

Meanwhile, the story of Bath's Fire Watch was flowing placidly downhill. Infuriated with his inability to achieve anything worthwhile, Robinson resigned, but during working out his notice the very thing that he had wanted happened.

During the summer of 1941, Minister of Home Security, Herbert Morrison, changed the name of the organisation from Fire Watch to Fire Guard and announced that taking part would be compulsory. There would be exemptions for various classes of people, namely those already undertaking work of national importance: Air Raid Warden, Home Guard etc. This meant, however, that it would generate a lot of paperwork. The expectation was that Major Lock would transfer some of his more experienced civil defence officers to the Fire Guard, but instead an advert was placed in the *Daily Telegraph*. Out of the eighty-nine applicants, the two chosen were 50-year-old Charles Scott Welch, who became the Fire Guard Staff Officer, and 43-year-old William Clarke, who would be his deputy.

Up until this point, there had been more than 1,000 fire brigades in Britain, with different command structures and different equipment. Under wartime conditions this clearly could not continue and so, on 18 August 1941, the Auxiliary Fire Service and all the local brigades were amalgamated to become the National Fire Service. The country was divided into regions which were sub-divided into forces. Bath came under Fire Force 17 within Region 7. Fire Force 17 had six divisions – A to F – and Bath was D Division.

Four schools and the Labour Exchange were used as Fire Guard registration centres. The registration days were Sunday, 14 September, Saturday, 20 September, and Sunday, 21 September. 15,000 people registered; some 5,000 fewer than had been expected.

Charles Scott Welch and his second-in-command, William Clarke, took up their posts at 2 Broad Street on Monday, 15 September, the Fire Guard Office being in the same building as the Warden's Office. Welch's intention was to build a proper command structure for the Fire Guard, so that personnel could report the situations which confronted them and also receive orders; however, the Fire Guard Office received so much paperwork in the form of applications for exemption from Fire Guard duty that there was simply no chance of doing so. Many of these came from Irish labourers engaged in building the Ammunition Depot at Monkton Farleigh. They were billeted in Bath but claimed exemption because they were engaged on work of national importance. There were so many of them that the Fire Guard Office was swamped with paperwork.

In October 1941, Bath's Air Raid Precautions Committee was renamed the Civil Defence Committee. Around this time 15,000 'Fire Guard' armlets were received and put into store. In a supreme irony, these would be destroyed when the building in which they were stored caught fire and was burnt to the ground.

The Business Premises Fire Prevention 1941 Order No.2 was introduced, which set a level of pay of 3s for a 12-hour shift outside normal hours, the payments being grant-aided by the government. This meant, however, that a register had to be compiled of all the premises under the scheme, to enable the council to reclaim the money that they had paid out to the businesses. The compilation of this register also fell to the Fire Guard Office which, with just Welch, Clarke and two secretaries, was already understaffed for the work they had to undertake. The register was never compiled.

And then, somewhat inexplicably, on Friday, 12 December 1941, Major Pickard, the city's coordinator of civil defence services, transferred William Clarke from the Fire Guard Office to be his own deputy. This made the staff shortage even worse. Welch and his two secretaries were trying to deal with a flood of paperwork meaning, inevitably, that there was no time to build an organisation capable, when the time came, of saving Bath from devastation by fire.

On 18 March 1942 the Bath City Treasurer wrote to the town clerk to state that the city's finances were getting into a parlous condition. What was happening was that the council's Treasury Department was making payments to businesses for Fire Guard duties but was unable to reclaim the money from central government until an up-to-date registration list could be supplied by the Fire Guard Office. By now the payments were two months in arrears.

Five days later, a meeting of the Emergency Committee was held to discuss the situation. So serious was it considered that the same day another meeting was held, this time at the police station in Orange Grove. It was considered that the Warden's organisation and the Fire Guard should be reorganised to come under the same control. A week later, 30 March, as part of the civil defence reorganisation, the Emergency Committee asked Welch to resign, which he did the following day. His replacement, on a temporary basis, was Senior Fire Guard Officer Gardner. This would be announced in the *Bath Chronicle* of 25 April, the day of the first air raid. After only a month in the job, Gardner would be plunged into the maelstrom of a heavy raid.

On 20 April, the regional team arrived to inspect Bath's firebomb defences. Assured by Lock that everything was in control, they later spoke to Gardner on his own who gave them a conflicting, and evidently most worrying report. He told them he had been unable to organise any leaders for the Fire Guard because his office was fully employed dealing with all the exemption certificates. This was why the register had not been completed and the city's finances were in such a mess. There was also no time for personnel to send in reports about what was happening on the ground and receive orders. Although this was not a problem peculiar to Bath – across the country there was far more work to be done than there were people to do it – with the decision-making power of Bath's entire civil defence organisation in the hands of effectively just one man, this created something of a unique problem.

This one man was Major Geoffrey Lock MC. Not only was he one of the two permanent members of the 'Big Three' of the Emergency Committee (the third, that of the mayor, was obviously open to personnel changes) he was also a councillor, chief warden – with 900 wardens under his command – and chairman of the ARP. This gave him a monopoly in the most vital aspects of the city's defence control and a potential for conflicts of interest. 'Popular politics and the needs of war were often in conflict at national level and equally manifested themselves locally,' states Scott, '[and this] uncomfortable mixture appeared in the reluctance to bring in blanket compulsion.'

Ultimately, those holding the power of the city's civil defence failed in their duty, not making either timely or correct decisions when required to do so. This led, according to Scott, 'into a distinct pattern of parochialism where outside influences and outsiders went through an ordeal by failure to vindicate political vanities.' The real losers of this situation were the 417 men, women and children who lost their lives over that weekend in April 1942.

In June 1942, Major Lock issued his Heads of Services Report. It is a self-damning analysis that is the complete anthesis of the document he showed the regional team back in April. In this later one he admits the failings of the Fire Guard and indeed of his own command. Possibly what is most damning, other than the fact that none of these failings were ever made public, is that the report was able to account to the last man who had died during the raids within the warden's organisation, but through lack of any paperwork, was unable to do the same for those killed on fire guard duty. As a postscript to this sorry tale, Major Lock would later be given an MBE.

CHAPTER 8

Crime, Convoys & Courage
(June 1942 to May 1943)

If 'bombed, bloodied and broken' was the state in which the people of Bath were meant to be left by the raids of April 1942, then the Germans were to be disappointed. Although the first two were almost inevitable, the last one was not. The *Bath Chronicle*, on the front page of its 2 May 1942 edition, was resolute that the attack had not 'broken' the city but only 'strengthened the resolve of the citizens to play their part in purging the world from the evil thing that is befouling all humanity.'

Despite this defiant attitude and the altruistic behaviour constantly in evidence in the aftermath of the raids, there were also less palatable, more disquieting aspects to surface from the Bath Blitz. Perhaps the most deplorable of these was looting, the unlawful taking of possessions from the bombed-out buildings which now pockmarked the city landscape or, even more heinous, the stealing from corpses as they lay half-buried in the rubble.

The royal visit the week after the raids.

Children playing in Julian Road.

In the city's defence, most looting cases involved outsiders, but still this contemptible act was widespread. According to Julie Gardiner in her book *Wartime: Britain 1939-1945*, 'After raids on Sheffield in December 1940, two full days of the Assize Court sitting had to be devoted to hearing charges of looting. The remarks of the presiding judge unfortunately could have applied equally to London, Manchester, Liverpool, Birmingham, Glasgow . . . "When a great city is attacked by bombs on a heavy scale, numbers of houses and their contents are left exposed and deprived of their natural defences. Necessarily these are the homes of comparatively poor people, since they are by far the most numerous."'

Bath could now be added to the judge's list. Despite the chief constable saying that complaints of looting had been 'negligible', many cases appeared before local magistrates during the following month and into the summer. The first report appeared in the 7 May edition of the *Bath Chronicle*. The accused was a soldier, Eric Blakemore, whose crime was alleged to have been the theft of two rings belonging to 'some person, or persons unknown'. The crime was said to have occurred on 29 April, two days after the third and final raid. The 24-year-old pleaded guilty to stealing both the rings, one diamond and the other gold. His case was linked to that of another soldier – David John Mitchell, an army sergeant of similar age – who appeared at the same Bath Quarter Sessions in connection with half a dozen charges of looting. But whereas Mitchell was sentenced to

The aftermath of the raids, with salvaged possessions on the street.

twelve months' imprisonment, Blakemore – who had served in France for three months and had been in the Dunkirk evacuation – was merely bound over for twelve months.

A 20-year-old carpenter's labourer required an interpreter when appearing in court charged with two thefts from bomb-damaged houses in the city. In spite of being deaf and dumb, Edwin Sheppard, of no fixed abode, requested six other offences to be taken into consideration and no doubt these, along with several previous convictions, contributed to the relatively harsh sentence he received of two years' hard labour, which was no doubt conveyed to Sheppard by his appointed signer, Reverend W. J. Freeman.

Perhaps a little more disturbing was the case of three local boys, two aged 13 and one of 12, who appeared at Bath Juvenile Court in July. They admitted that they had entered a bomb-damaged house in Lansdown the previous month and taken a silver watch, a sword and a sheath knife, among other items, worth £9 5s in total. Having been found guilty, two of the boys were bound over for twelve months and ordered to pay 15s costs, while the third – with previous convictions – was sent to a training school. Another trio of boys were also placed on a year's probation for stealing wheels off a truck and taking a toy motor-car; the youngest of these boys was 11.

And then there were the rumours, which spread around the city like Chinese whispers. One concerned members of the Home Guard, now in possession of live ammunition, who it was said had shot dead a looter. The truth was that this had become standard practice – the carrying of live ammunition, that is, not the fatal shooting of looters (this was more the *modus operandi* in Germany).

*Helping to feed those
left without homes.*

Those involved in the clearing-up process were not above temptation, as in the case of Thomas Pitcher who appeared at Bath Police Court in August 1942. Pitcher was involved in the demolition of bombed-out houses in the city of Bath. On his return home to Hackney, he was arrested at Paddington Station after two large packages he was carrying aroused the suspicion of police officers. Investigating, they found 'a variety of articles' that had come from properties in the Oldfield Park area. The 41-year-old was sentenced to six months' imprisonment for his crime.

Reginald Ernest Baker from Bridgwater had been on demolition and haulage work in Bath when 'sudden temptation' had led him to take two bomb-damaged clocks from rubble he had been transporting to the tip. Although when the case came to court, the 29-year-old also asked for a further charge of stealing three pewter bowls, a tankard and a jug to be taken in consideration by the bench. Despite these charges being 'found proved', Bath magistrates considered the fact Baker had been at Dunkirk, along with evidence from his wife regarding the subsequent effect on his health of his service. He was fined £10.

Another rumour, although finding its way into the official record, was that a 'rescue squad' had entered the city from elsewhere but had taken no part in the rescue operation. The idea of 'organised' gangs coming down from London was not beyond the realms of possibility and indeed there had been at least one occurrence elsewhere. Gardiner cites the case of Dover which, having been largely evacuated in the summer of 1940 after finding itself in the front line of a German attack, suffered from the attention of unscrupulous gangs from London. But as the author makes clear, these consisted of pre-war pickpockets and petty criminals. Professional gangs stayed clear of this activity; not out of any patriotic duty, but because their main targets – large country houses potentially full of jewellery, valuable antiques and art treasures that had not been hidden underground somewhere else – were much more profitable.

One man who probably did find himself up against a gang 'down from London' was Twerton resident Eric Davies. Davies and his family were at home in Eleanor Place during the first night of the blitz, when two bombs fell in the field behind their house and they were caught in the blast. Although there were no fatalities, their property had become unsafe and so they left to stay elsewhere. His post-bombing experience is recounted in *The Bombing of Bath* by Niall Rothnie:

"I lost everything in the blitz . . . we lost every stick of furniture, bar one chair. No one could find anything – not even my gun. I had to verify it was gone with the local police at Twerton, so that I could get new army kit.

"My brother got a bath out of our home. He salvaged some other goods from the house, put them in the bath and covered them with a rug. But a dress and other things and ornaments were taken from there. The people who took them were from London. My uncle was in a pub and heard them arranging for transport and when the lorry would pick the stuff up. They'd taken our stuff, and others, to Clyde Buildings. My uncle heard there was stuff in that house already and it was going to London. I contacted the CID and they sent two men down. We went to the house and a detective forced the lock. In the house I recognised a clock which was the landlord's. He wasn't interested, but I was incensed. What we'd dug out in the bath was gone.

"But the men claimed they'd dug me out. I had no witnesses. The people swore they helped dig us out. I didn't want to take action if they had helped rescue me. I later found out they hadn't, but I was on the spot. Then, I didn't know who dug us out. We found the dress. One of their wives was wearing the dress in an East End pub. It was a big bit in the paper at the time. I seemed the villain of the piece. My wife got her dress back and a couple of saucepans and other things."

A local paper carried the story of the trial under the heading: 'Blitz heroine on loot charge'. It reported that the woman had been given the bath by workers at the site as she wanted it for her children. The dress had been thrown to her. This and other items in the bath were taken to a house in Clyde Buildings. She claimed her husband knew nothing of this. She also presented other peoples' testimonies as to her bravery in helping to rescue people. Suitably impressed, the bench had said there were 'special circumstances' in this case and she was merely bound over to appear for judgment, if recalled, in the next 12 months. Some of the goods were returned. The woman was not recalled and had no further punishment.

Mr Davies eventually received £12 from the mayor's fund towards the cost of replacing part of his lost property, but no doubt the whole episode added an unpleasant note to the traumatic experience which had started it all; that of being bombed out of one's own home.

If most were innocent of the more despicable crimes such as looting, many nevertheless became lawbreakers almost inadvertently. Whether it was accidentally leaving a chink in their curtains during blackout, forgetting to take their ID card on a quick trip to the shops, or not realising they had the wrong kind of masking on the headlamps of their car, all these situations, and countless others, were punishable by law, thus making criminals out of the perpetrators – normally law-abiding citizens in peacetime. Given all these new opportunities to break the law, many of which had been put on the wartime statue book by the Emergency Powers (Defence) Bill passed on 24 August 1939, and which continued to be added to on a regular basis through the war, it is hardly surprising to find that the 303,771 'crimes' which were committed nationwide in 1939 had risen 57 per cent to 478,394 in 1945.

Other 'crimes' included the butcher who kept 'a little back under the counter' for favoured customers, users of dead relatives' ration books, builders of sub-standard air-raid shelters, and even those not shy about selling 'coupon' items at higher prices but without any coupons changing hands.

Then, of course, there were the acts of criminality committed by those who knew exactly what they were doing and had been doing so deliberately since before the war: the habitual thieves, calculating con-men, cold-blooded murderers and the downright hardened villains, all of whom had made their livings off the proceeds of their crimes in peacetime and now used the war as an opportunity to continue their nefarious acts. The blackout and the blitz offered excellent cover, although obviously both brought with them certain occupational hazards.

Sometimes there is a tendency to view the home front in the war through rose-tinted spectacles where communities helped each other out, where people were more honest, and crime did not exist. Bath is no exception in this respect. But the truth is that Bath experienced its fair share of theft, assault, child abuse, joy-riding, juvenile crime, and all the other anti-social behaviours and misdemeanours which make up any urbanised society either then or now. There is probably not a crime-related story which might appear in a current issue of the *Bath Chronicle* that could not find a counterpart within the pages of its wartime editions. On 22 April 1940, for example, a report appeared of three youths (aged 19, 18 and 15) who were alleged to have stolen a car and driven it at speed around the city centre. When a police car set off in pursuit, the car thieves stopped their car at the top of a steep rise near Camden Crescent, jumped out without pulling on the handbrake and deliberately let it roll back into the path of the pursuing patrol car. The two older boys were residents of the Bath Lads' Home.

Other incidents of anti-social behaviour not unfamiliar to readers of the newspapers of today included 'mindless' acts of vandalism in the city parks, such as Victoria and Henrietta, life-buoys being maliciously thrown into the River Avon, under-age drinking on the city streets and an assault on a police officer by five youths, aged between 17 and 20. Underage sex was also a concern for local authorities – amplified by, although not confined to, the arrival of American soldiers from the summer of 1942 onwards. One example of this was a 14-year-old girl who was sent to an approved school for her nocturnal liaisons with GIs in a centre park.

There were violent acts – assault, even attempted murder and manslaughter – but these were rare and most deaths throughout this period resulted from natural causes, illnesses, accidents or the war. Incidents of rape and sexual assault were also rare, or at least did not appear often in the pages of the *Bath Chronicle*, and when they did, a lot of the time it was in relation to American GIs, specifically coloured ones. The most notorious was that of Leroy Henry, and such was the surrounding controversy it has been called 'arguably the most widely publicised and discussed single incident during the whole American presence in Britain.' The details of this case will be discussed in the following chapter.

Purveyors in the city of the black market – the illegal buying and selling of rationed or otherwise forbidden items – although operating throughout the war, found their services more sought after in the lead-up to major celebrations, such as Christmas and Easter. The reason it flourished was due to the scarcity of many of the required goods.

From the beginning of the war, Germany did all in its power to impose a naval blockade against Britain. In 1939, Britain was almost wholly dependent on imports of foodstuffs and raw materials and so it was essential that maritime channels remained open. Britain, however, had the largest maritime fleet in the world – around 4,000 vessels, to help protect it during the war. American ships also helped in various capacities. The main threat to Allied shipping came from German submarines, and in the first three years of the war a terrible toll was inflicted on the convoys that sailed across the North Atlantic. Hunting in packs, or alone, U-boats accounted for the sinking of 700,000 tons of shipping in April 1941 alone.

The loss of life was also great, both from the Royal and Merchant navies, and the need for personnel became dire. One man only too aware of the shortage of Merchant Navy seamen was 62-year-old widower John Charles Lewis, of 'Ivanhoe', Bloomfield Road, Bath. He had served as an engineer in the Merchant

Navy during the First World War and despite being torpedoed four times, had survived. Although spending most of his life in Wales, he had come to live with his sister in Bath two years before, after the death of his wife. Against the wishes of this sister, he had rejoined his ship towards the end of 1940: 'They're needing engineers very badly', he had told her. Although surviving a further two torpedo attacks, John Lewis's luck ran out six weeks after he had gone back afloat. His name appears on the merchant shipping fatal casualty list, dated February 1941.

The situation worsened despite America joining the war, and during October and November 1942 nearly 240 ships were sunk. In January 1943, Petty Officer Reginald Legg, of Kingsmead East, was reported 'missing believed killed in a recent action'. Legg had been serving with the destroyer HMS *Firedrake*, engaged on North Atlantic convoy protection duties, and during the night of 17 December 1942, 600 miles south of Iceland and in mountainous seas, *Firedrake* was torpedoed and sunk by a German U-boat.

Reginald Legg distinguished himself throughout the war and indeed had been awarded the Distinguished Service Medal for his actions during the evacuation of Dunkirk back in June 1940. At the time Leading Seaman Legg was 'a crewman on HM Skoot *Twente* [according to the Falconers' book, 'a skoot is a shallow draught coastal craft, not unlike a Thames barge in appearance']. The *Twente* left Ramsgate on 28 May and made its way across the Channel to Dunkirk. For the next three days

Legg and his fellow crew members went back and forth, ferrying more than 1,500 troops to safety, in very demanding circumstances and enduring frequent air attacks. It was during the first full day the *Twente* was helping with the evacuation that the incident occurred in which Reginald Legg won his DSM. HMS *Gracie Fields*, with 750 troops on board, became a sitting target after being bombed by enemy aircraft. Enduring frequent Stuka dive-bombing attacks, and the ship's broken pipes gushing out scalding steam, HM Skoots *Twente* and *Jutland* nevertheless tied up alongside the larger ship and successfully transferred the soldiers across. The Navy's official citation read,

Reginald Legg who was a Dunkirk hero but lost his life later on HMS Firedrake.

Leading   Seaman   Reginald   Legg displayed coolness and resource under fire during the several trips as coxswain of the *Twente* and later in the motor launch *Kestrel*. He was largely responsible for the successful rescues from the sinking *Gracie Fields* by his seamanlike actions. His conduct at all times was admirable.

A few months into 1943, due to the increased effectiveness of Allied countermeasures – such as Ultra intelligence and new technical and tactical innovations to protect the convoys – U-boat losses rose significantly while convoy losses dropped dramatically. Added to the latter was, by now, the enormous expansion of the US shipping industry.

Towards the end of 1943, another Bath man became involved in a naval action that would result in an award. On Boxing Day, engaged in convoy protection off the Norwegian coast, Captain Frederick Parham, of 18 Sion Hill, was in command of heavy cruiser HMS *Belfast*, when it sighted the battle cruiser *Scharnhorst*. This German ship had been responsible for the sinking of HMS *Rawalpindi* and HMS *Glorious* as well as many others, resulting in the deaths of Douglas Farrant and others. The *Bath Chronicle* later gave an account of the subsequent events through the words of the commander himself. According to Captain Parham, the entire action had consisted of three phases. 'The first was brief, we made contact with a large unidentified vessel which was obviously the *Scharnhorst* and [HMS] *Norfolk* opened fire, while we fired star shells. The enemy did not return the fire and eventually sheered off.' Captain Parham then decided to return to the convoy in case the *Scharnhorst* tried to attack it. This is exactly what happened, as when they returned to their position on the convoy's bow, contact was made again. Three HMS cruisers – *Belfast, Norfolk* and *Duke of York* – opened fire and after the squadron turned in line abreast head-on to the enemy, they 'rode at him at full speed'. Captain Parham then described the third and final stage: 'For a moment it looked as if the *Scharnhorst* was going to stand and fight. Then he appeared to lose his nerve, and turned tail and fled. The cruisers followed after him, and both sides were firing away with their main armament. Red points of light showed that we were scoring hits. It was this time that the *Norfolk* was hit. No shots fell near us and only the flashes of her guns told us that the *Scharnhorst* was firing. What we had prayed for was happening. The *Scharnhorst* was sailing away from the convoy – and (what she did not know) running straight into the arms of the *Duke of York*.'

In the atrocious bitter cold, rough artic seas and paling daylight, *Scharnhorst* finally met its dramatic end. Heavily fired upon by HMS *Belfast* and *Duke of York*, as well as torpedoed by supporting destroyers, the German ship finally exploded and slid beneath the dark and icy waters. Nearly 2,000 of its crew were lost and there were only thirty-six survivors. For his participation in this action, Captain Parham was awarded the DSO. He would later be knighted and become an admiral.

As well as playing their part in the dangerous North Atlantic convoy runs, merchant and royal navy personnel from Bath were involved in the transportation of aid to Russia, to try to keep the country in the war against its former ally, Germany. Two of these men – Lance Sergeant Bert Smith and Gunner Frank Brown, both in the Maritime AA – ended up in the pages of the *Bath Chronicle* after a somewhat chilling experience, literally. The pair had sailed in the same convoy from Iceland in June 1942, heading for the Russian port of Arkhangelsk. Somewhere during this journey, due to an error by higher command, the merchant ships of convoy PQ17 found themselves without any Royal Navy protection. Alone and scattered throughout the Barents Sea, 400 miles north of the Artic Circle, the ships became easy targets for U-boats and German dive-bombers and after four days of continuous attacks twenty-three of them had been dispatched to the bottom of the ocean. Although Smith and Brown survived the sinking of their ships, they now found themselves together in an open boat, along with thirty-six other men, in freezing conditions and with only biscuits to sustain them. Their ordeal lasted eight days before they were picked up by a local trawler. Frank Brown, of 3 Shaftesbury Avenue, Lower Weston, spent four weeks in a Russian hospital before returning home, while Lance Sergeant Bert Smith, of 9 Grove Street, Bath, was later awarded the DSM for his devotion to duty.

In 1943, Bath gained a second airfield, situated on a relatively unusual site: a racecourse. RAF Charmy Down had been purpose built on fields to the north-east of the city, this one was to the north-west. Horse racing had taken place in Bath from the eighteenth century onwards, although its main racecourse had moved during the Napoleonic Wars from its original home at Claverton Down right across the city to the other side up onto Lansdown. When it initially relocated there, the course was sited between Beckford's Tower and Weston Lane, before finding its now permanent fixture further along the great expanse of land owned by the Blathwayt family.

The Lansdown site was inspected as a potential airfield by the Air Ministry in May 1943. Although meetings were held there during the first year of the war, there had not been any since May 1940, around the time the War Office requisitioned part of it for their use, but the ground not being used by the War Office had been maintained to a reasonable condition. The purpose for the new airfield, once the site was green-lighted by Wing Commander Gosnell, the commanding officer of 3 Flying Instructors School (Advanced) (FIS(A)), was as a landing ground for his unit.

'The course railings were removed, and after minimal preparation a runway was laid out on the grass in an east-west alignment,' according to David Berryman in his book on Somerset airfields in the Second World War, and 'alternative landing and take-off runs were marked for secondary use.' The new airfield was named North Stoke. Soon 'student pilots of 3 FIS(A) were to be seen flying their aircraft from the new landing ground. These were mainly Airspeed Oxford twin-engine trainers, but the single-engine trainers also flown by the unit, such as the North American Harvard, Miles Magister, and Miles Master were occasionally to be seen at North Stoke. The school moved to Lulsgate Bottom in early October 1943 but continued to use North Stoke as its relief landing ground.'

Although termed 'students', the pilots, as the unit's title suggested, were well-qualified. This was just as well, as the woods bordering two sides of the airfield, which stood on the edge of a plateau, meant it could be a difficult place from which to operate. A serious incident occurred in early March 1945 when an Oxford was badly damaged on landing, but other than that, there were only a few other minor ones.

Even though there had been no airfields in Bath before the Second World War, the connection between Bath and the Royal Air Force had always been strong, ever since the latter's inception towards the end of the First World War, in 1917. Bath had seen several of its young men join the Royal Flying Corps as it was known then (many to become the fathers of Second World War RAF pilots) and several had died and also achieved awards for their bravery.

In this war the bravery continued, and many heroic deeds were performed by the fighter aces of 'the few' who came from Bath. Numerous 'aerial heroes' saw their actions acknowledged through medals, while others no less heroic remained largely unsung outside their immediate family and close associates.

One of these was 21-year-old Pilot Officer Hilary Patrick Edridge, who died at the end of October 1940 during the Battle of Britain when his Spitfire crashed after an encounter with a Bf109. Although pulled from the blazing wreckage alive, he died of his injuries. His death occurred on the penultimate day of

Hilary Edridge, the 21-year-old Spitfire pilot who lost his life during the Battle of Britain.

the battle's official end and so he was one of the last, if not *the* last, of the 537 'few' who lost their lives. He was born in 1919 and at the time of his death his family lived at No.29 Gay Street in Bath. He attended Stonyhurst College and afterwards held a commission with the 4th Battalion Somerset Light Infantry. He had taken a short service commission in the RAF two years earlier and, as well as being involved in the Battle of Britain, with 222 Squadron, had also fought over Dunkirk during the evacuation of the BEF. Among his 'kills' was a Bf109 which he had shot down at this time; he also shared in the destruction of a Bf110 ten days before he was killed. He had been downed at least once before, back in August 1940 over Kent, when he baled out with burns to his face. A Requiem Mass was held for him at St Mary's Roman Catholic Church in Julian Road, before his burial took place across the city at Perrymead Cemetery. Six RAF sergeants acted as pall-bearers, and an escort party formed a guard of honour from the gates of the cemetery to the graveside. A volley of shots gave the salute and the *Last Post* and the *Reveille* were sounded during the ceremony.

The most decorated and highest scoring night-fighter pilot of the entire war was another local man, who came from the village of Holcombe, near Bath. Wing

The grave of Pilot Officer Edridge at Perrymead, Bath – one of the 'few'.

Commander Bob Braham DSO*, DFC*, was the son of a Methodist minister in the city but grew up to become one of the deadliest practitioners of the art of night-fighting. His total of twenty-nine enemy aircraft destroyed and numerous medals (three DSOs and three DFCs) are a testament to this. He flew Bristol Beaufighters and later De Havilland Mosquitos, while attached to 29 and 141 squadrons. He spent the last few months of the war as a prisoner-of-war, after being shot down not long after D-Day.

Squadron Leader James Maclachlan DSO DFC* did not survive the war. His career during the conflict was perhaps one of the most varied of the pilots who had connection with the city or surrounding areas. He saw action in France during the summer of 1940 as a bomber pilot but transferred to Fighter Command in June, just in time to play his part in the Battle of Britain. An overseas posting to the besieged island of Malta followed, where he claimed eight enemy aircraft in one month! His forearm was amputated after a run-in with a German fighter who downed him in February 1941. Although operated on, his left arm had been too shattered by cannon shell and the doctors' efforts were in vain. This did not stop him flying, however, and within a month he was back in the air. By the time he returned to England, he had command of 1 Squadron and had been fitted with an artificial limb. In June 1943, Maclachlan joined the Air Fighting Development Unit, where he flew sorties in North American Mustang fighters. One of these resulted in a ten-minute dog-fight south of Paris in which, along with a fellow Mustang pilot, they shot down half a dozen enemy planes. Another sortie the following month however, resulted in the Old Monktonian crash-landing his burning aircraft in a field near Dieppe and dying of his injuries in a German hospital a few days later.

The flamboyant escapades of Wing Commander Johnny Baldwin DSO* DFC* included the chasing of German aircraft around the Eiffel Tower in January 1944 and leading a group of Typhoons later that year that were possibly responsible for wounding Field Marshal Erwin 'Desert Fox' Rommel. Baldwin's family was bombed out of their Bath home in Green Park during the Bath Blitz and, although the wing commander survived the war, he was posted missing in action seven years later during the Korean one. His fate remains unknown to this day.

Mention should also be made of Squadron Leader Lewis Brandon DSO DFC*, Flight Lieutenant R.F.W. Turner DFC, Pilot Officer J.H. Toone DFC, and Sergeant William Mulliss.

Brandon was dubbed 'Donat's Double' in the press, as the Bath man had appeared many times as actor Robert Donat's screen stand-in, including in the 1939 classic *Goodbye Mr Chips*. He was part of a successful RAF night-fighter crew, first on home defence duties, then later on night-fighter patrols and intruder sorties into occupied Europe. He received many awards for his bravery, survived the war, and wrote about the experience in a book entitled *Night Flyer*.

R.F.W. Turner survived the war. He accumulated a wealth of operational experience, and bravery awards, as a rear gunner in a Lancaster before being shot down with the rest of his crew in August 1943. Ending up as a prisoner-of-war in the notorious Stalag Luft 3 camp, he took part in the 'Great Escape' and, although unsuccessful in his attempt at freedom, lived to tell the tale (fifty of the seventy-six men who escaped were recaptured and shot dead in cold blood by the Gestapo). The camp was liberated in April 1945 and he returned to his home in Bath – 27 Royal Crescent – the following month.

Pilot Officer Toone was killed in a flying accident in November 1942. He was making a name for himself as half of a night-fighter duo – dubbed 'Salt and Pepper' – that had in the month they died shot down three enemy raiders in one night (up to that point only the second hat-trick of the war). The other half of the team was Flying Officer George Pepper DFC. Toone had been a director of a well-known provisions store in Bath – Sydney W. Bush & Son – and it was not long before he was rechristened 'Salt'. Toone, of 13 Hensley Road, was awarded the DFC for his part in the hat-trick, but by the time it was officially announced he was dead.

Although Thomas Gray is the only name on Bath's official memorial with the letters VC engraved after it, there is another on it whose actions were deemed similarly worthy of receiving this highest order but who was ultimately denied it. RAF Sergeant William Cecil Mulliss of 30 Charlcombe Lane, Larkhall, was part of a four-man crew of a Coastal Command Beaufort detailed to attack the German battle-cruiser *Gneisenau* in Brest Harbour at dawn on 6 April 1941. The ship was heavily protected and there was almost no chance of returning alive, as the low-level attack required to deliver a successful blow would not allow the rapidly rising ground beyond to be cleared without crashing into it. Flying Officer Kenneth Campbell and the rest of this 'suicide' crew, including Sergeant Mulliss, from 22 Squadron RAFVR, nevertheless 'went cheerfully and resolutely to the task'. As a result of the attack, the battle-cruiser was severely damaged below the waterline and subsequently put out of action for nine months. As expected, the aircraft crashed immediately afterwards, killing the crew.

Eleven months later, enough evidence had been collected to warrant the VC being given. The award as a posthumous decoration however, can only be given to one member of a crew and so Flying Officer Kenneth Campbell received it in respect of the rest of the crew. Although nobody would doubt that Thomas Gray was worthy of his award, he was in fact dead when his VC was awarded but officially reported as 'missing'. If the award had been delayed like this one, and given posthumously, then no doubt Donald Garland, as the flying officer of the crew, would have received it and not Gray.

William Mulliss's widow had now suffered a double bereavement as her brother Henry (her maiden name was Pickford) had been killed by the bomb at Charmy Down back in August 1940.

CHAPTER 9

'Over Here' to Overlord (June 1943 – June 1944)

By the end of 1943, it felt in the city, even from the meagre scraps of uncensored news its citizens had access to, that the tide was turning. There had been stunning victories in North Africa, convoy losses in the North Atlantic had substantially decreased, Italy had been invaded and taken out of the war, and shiploads of troops and equipment were making the journey across the Atlantic and then heading towards the south coast of England – suggesting something big was being planned. As it transpired, this was to be Operation Overlord – the Allied invasion of France – with the operation landings to take place on the Normandy beaches. This would be the biggest amphibious invasion undertaken in the history of warfare and is today more commonly known as D-Day. One of the obstacles that had to be overcome was the absence of a port or harbour at the places chosen to land the troops. A harbour invasion had been attempted at Dieppe in 1942 and had been a disaster – although lessons had been learnt. To successfully invade, it was understood that a harbour would need to be found and the solution was one of the most remarkable feats of this, or indeed any, war.

The Allies decided they would build their own harbour – in parts – ship it across the channel and reassemble it on the French shoreline. The task of designing the harbour was given to a department of the Admiralty that was stationed at Kingswood School on the northern slope of Bath near Lansdown. A name was required for the harbour and local legend has it that when the chief engineer was thinking of a name, he looked out of the window and seeing the mulberry tree which grew near his window, the harbour was duly given that name. According to the school's own website though, the fact a tree was growing there was sheer coincidence: the harbour was named Mulberry as this was simply the next codename on the list.

Although the tide did indeed seem to be turning, the loss of allied lives remained high. Towards late September 1943, for example, two 'River' Class Frigates were sunk by U-boats in quick succession, each frigate with a Bath man on board. Colin Richardson, an 18-year-old assistant cook was killed when HMS *Lagan* was torpedoed by U-270 on 20 September, while three days later,

HMS *Itchen* was sunk while on duty in the North Atlantic by U-666. One of her crew was 19-year-old Clifford Waldron. Both men are commemorated on the Plymouth Naval Memorial.

The following month another Bath man died. This was Joseph William Russell, a private in the 4th Suffolk Regiment. His death was not caused by a U-boat, but through one of the darkest episodes of not just the Second World War, but the whole of human history; namely the Japanese treatment of their prisoners of war (POWs).

Many of the men taken prisoner when Singapore surrendered were put to work by the Japanese on the now infamous Burma-Thailand Railway. This was a metre-gauge (3' 3") line which the Japanese wanted to build through the mountains and jungles straddling the border between the two countries to avoid the long and dangerous sea voyage around the Malay Peninsula. The line was 415 km (258 miles) long, and ran from Thanbyuzayat, on the Rangoon–Ye Line in Burma, to Bampong on the Bangkok–Singapore Line in Thailand (then called Siam). To put it into perspective, it is about the distance between London Paddington and Redruth in Cornwall, going via Westbury. It was built with the most basic tools imaginable and with total disregard for human life. It was begun in September 1942 and followed a route that British engineers, surveying the area in 1910, had ruled out as too difficult. The intended completion date, nevertheless, was set for Saturday, 16 October 1943.

Throughout the remaining months of 1942 and into 1943 the work progressed, with many allied lives, many from Bath, being lost through complete exhaustion, emaciation or disease. It is said that on the most difficult sections of the route one life was lost for every sleeper that was laid. Even worse was to come, however. As the two halves of the line approached each other the Japanese engineers adopted what they called 'Speedo' tactics, forcing their prisoners to work even more impossible hours to get the job finished. When a worker died they were normally buried nearby, but after the war many of these individual burials were disinterred and transferred to two large war cemeteries; Thanbyuzayat in Burma (3,149 dead) and Kanchanaburi in Thailand (4,946 dead). Those whose bodies could not be found, or identified, are remembered on the Singapore Memorial.

One of the Bath men who died was William Henry Combstock, a 41-year-old driver in the Royal Corps of Signals. Taken prisoner by the Japanese, he was put to work on the railway. The barbaric treatment which he received no doubt caused him to pass away on Tuesday, 3 August 1943. He was buried at Kanchanaburi and was husband to Elsie. Also, on the same day, 28-year-old William George Lumber died. He was a private in the RAOC and as well as being the son of David and Ellen Lumber, he was husband to Annie. He is buried in the Allied War Cemetery at Thanbyuzayat. By the time 27-year-old Joseph William Russell died, on

9 October 1943, it was just one week before the lines met, and so it is almost certain that his death was the result of one of the 'Speedo' pushes that the Japanese resorted to in order to get the line finished on time. He is also buried at Thanbyuzayat.

Arthur Frank Fry was a 29-year-old flight sergeant in No. 434 Squadron of the Royal Air Force when he died on the 23 of October, as did John Francis Grant, from Lansdown, Bath. The 33-year-old had been a stoker onboard the 'Dido Class' cruiser HMS *Charybdis* when it was sunk attempting to intercept the German blockade-runner 'Munsterland'. The following day, HMS *Eclipse* was sunk by a mine. The destroyer had been in the Aegean Sea, east of the island of Kalymnos. On hitting the mine, she broke in two and sank within five minutes. One-hundred-and-nineteen of her crew were killed including two men from Bath; Ordinary Seaman George Albert Booker and Supply Assistant Edward George Rice. They are both commemorated on the Plymouth Naval Memorial. Four days later, John Rodger, a 28-year-old lance sergeant in the 2/7th Battalion, The Queen's Royal Regiment (West Surrey) was killed in Italy. He is buried in the Allied War Cemetery at Minturno.

The rest of the 1943 continued in the same, sad vein. Reginald Horace Hopkins came from Combe Down in Bath. The 41-year-old had been a stoker on the 'Dragonfly' class River Gunboat HMS *Grasshopper*. The ship had been sunk on Valentine's Day the previous year and he was taken prisoner by the Japanese. Although the railway was now completed, he died on 22 November and is buried at Thanbyuzayat. Exactly one week later, Gordon Leslie McLoughlin Jones also died. He was 21, the son of Charles and Alice and an aircraftsman 1st Class in the Royal Air Force. He is remembered on the Singapore Memorial. Not all Bath men taken prisoner by the Japanese succumbed to their ordeal at the time though. Two men who came home were G.A. Collier of Bailbrook Grove, Lower Swainswick (although sadly he only lived a short while after his return) and Harold Temblett of Cranmore Place, Odd Down. Fascinatingly, a letter the latter had sent from his prison camp to home now resides in the Bath Postal Museum.

Earlier in the month, on Sunday, 7 November, Robert William Patch died. He was 23 and a sergeant in the RAF No. 285 Squadron. This squadron was based at RAF Woodvale, near Formby in Lancashire, and operated aircraft for Anti-Aircraft Co-operation purposes. He is buried at Haycombe Cemetery, in Bath: Plot 39; Section H; Row A; Grave 255. Many years later, a relative, Henry John 'Harry' Patch, would become 'the Last Fighting Tommy' of the First World War. Born at Combe Down, in Bath, 'Harry' Patch spent the Second World War as an Auxiliary Fireman because, in his own words, 'he was too old to be conscripted'.

The final month of 1943 saw another ship lost and another Bath man killed. HMS *Tynedale* was a 'Hunt' Class Destroyer. On Sunday, 12 December she was escorting convoy KMS34 off the coast of Algeria when she was torpedoed by the German submarine U-593. Like HMS *Eclipse*, two months earlier, she broke in two and sank. Out of the 146 crew on board, exactly half of them were killed, including Leading Seaman Henry Hefferman from Weston. His name is recorded on the Plymouth Naval Memorial.

The casualties continued into the New Year, with numerous deaths of Bath men being recorded throughout all the major theatres of the war. These included 32-year-old Gunner George August Frederick Baatz, at Cassino, in Italy, William Leonard Greenman, a 24-year-old corporal in the 2nd Battalion of the Somerset Light Infantry in Egypt, RAF Flight Sergeant (Wireless Operator) Charles John Geoffrey Wilce of No.57 Squadron in Poland, and 31-year-old Corporal William Henry Dagger, in India. Also dying in the latter country was 23-year-old Private Dennis John Cowley. All these Bath men died in January 1944.

Although by the beginning of 1944, Italy had changed sides, German troops were still in Italy and fighting stubbornly. Victor Raymond Kelson was a

Above left: *144 Maintenance Unit, which the authors' Uncle Ron belonged, photographed in Brindisi, Italy.*

Above right: *The authors' Uncle Ron when stationed in Italy.*

23-year-old gunner in the 98th Field Regiment of the Royal Artillary. He died on Friday, 28 January and is buried in the Minturno War Cemetery, 78 km north of Naples. Exactly a week later, on Friday, 4 February Donald Abrahams died. He was a private in the 1st King's Own Yorkshire Light Infantry and is also buried at Minturno. He was the 21-year-old son of William and Florence of 9 Bailbrook Grove, Lower Swainswick. He is commemorated in Swainswick Church.

While all these casualties were occurring, the influx of soldiers from across the Atlantic continued unabated, although compared with many towns and cities in the south-west, Bath's influx of American GIs was almost non-existent. Although US Airmen were stationed temporarily at Charmy Down, renamed accordingly 'AAF Station No.487' during their stay, no American soldiers were billeted in Bath. Those who were spotted on its streets were usually either visiting from one of the US 1st Army bases dotted elsewhere, such as High Littleton, Blagdon and Beckington, or else they were one of the walking wounded being cared for up at the military hospital in Combe Park. The medical buildings adjacent to the Royal United Hospital had originally been built to be used by British forces but in August 1942 they were taken over by the Americans, at which time it became known as 152nd Station Hospital. The hospital comprised 14 wards and 394 beds and cared for and treated sick and wounded American military personnel located 'within a radius of approximately 50 miles of Bath'.

Halifax NA454 of No.148 Squadron, one of the planes the authors' Uncle Ron maintained.

Despite the absence of billeted GIs, this period in Bath's wartime history is not without controversy and two differing aspects of the city's character revealed themselves. The first related to what American soldiers perceived to be 'overcharging'. Although a Red Cross Club had opened at the Lansdown Grove Hotel in October 1942 to provide various comforts of home for American servicemen on leave in the city, many chose to stay elsewhere, such as in bed & breakfast establishments or hotels. The *Bath Chronicle*, however, was soon reporting the fact that many soldiers, spending their leave in Bath, 'are complaining that they are being defrauded by a small minority of Bath's hotel keepers and café proprietors who, they allege, demand extravagant prices.'

Bath was introduced to American GIs as early as mid-1942. Most of these were young men with little experience of the opposite sex or being away from home, but as their older, more sexually experienced comrades came over in the build up to D-Day, many brought with them a 'brashness' that rubbed the city's male population up the wrong way. They also brought a charm and exuberance – along with pocketfuls of treats and hard-to-find items such as nylons, chocolate, cigarettes and chewing gum – that endeared them to women and children. This further added to the resentment of the local men, especially those in the armed forces, and frequent fights in public houses around the city were the result.

But if there were conflicts between American and British soldiers, in Bath as elsewhere, then there seems to have been even fiercer ones between the US soldiers themselves – specifically between white and black. Segregation in America had existed ever since the abolishment of slavery back in the nineteenth century, and the civil rights movement would not truly make an impact until two decades hence. With segregation, of course, blacks and whites ate, slept and travelled in separate places, or else within separate sections in the same building or public transport. It was therefore a foregone conclusion that this state of affairs would cause ripples when transposed across the Atlantic. As segregation did not exist in Britain, this gave black American soldiers a freedom they had rarely, if ever, experienced; while at the same time causing resentment because of it from white ones and leading to potential violent confrontation. However, the US Army, with the co-operation of the British government, instigated a number of measures – almost unimaginable to us today – in order to counteract possible altercations; although many saw these as being prejudiced against the blacks. 'British people were shocked by the attitudes of the American Army towards black soldiers,' Felicity Hebditch suggests in *Somerset in the Second World War*. 'The [war] was supposed to be a fight for justice for all people and against Hitler's racist policies but the black soldiers were unfairly treated.' One of the most controversial was the programme of restricting the visiting of certain towns and villages to just one race – black or white – or the only marginally less contentious, alternative-day system. Both measures were widespread throughout Somerset, with Bath's near-neighbour Frome being the unwelcome recipient of the latter. This in effect meant that white American soldiers could only visit the historic market town on certain days, while blacks could seek R 'n' R on the others. As one white American soldier remembered years later, '[the policy] was all right until the white soldiers happened to ask their English girl friends who they went out with on the coloured nights.'

Underpinning this potentially volatile situation was the fact the Americans not only had their own military police force with them, nicknamed 'snow drops' due to their white hats, but also brought with them their own judicial system. They even had their own special cell at Bath police station where they could take troublesome American servicemen. It was best not to get on the wrong side of either – the police or the judicial system – especially, as it transpired, if you were black as, according to Julie Gardiner in her book *Wartime Britain*, 'It also became clear that more black GIs were prosecuted than white and that, if found guilty, they received longer and harsher sentences.' Gardiner continues by saying that the execution of several black GIs found guilty of rape led to disquiet in Parliament, and the question to be asked about 'whether rape was a capital offence only when committed by black GIs.' She then makes reference to the most notorious case of the war: that of Leroy Henry, which supposedly occurred in Bath. On 5 May 1944, a month before D-Day, it was alleged in military court that Leroy Henry, a black truck driver from Missouri but now an American GI stationed in England for the build up to the invasion of France, had visited a house in Combe Down. It was late in the night and he had asked directions back to his barracks. A 33-year-old woman, in bed with her husband when Henry had knocked on their cottage, first provided directions and then went with the American GI to show him the way, after he asked her to do so. As they walked along, the woman pointing out the way he should go, he allegedly pulled a knife and demanded sex, threatening to kill her if she was not agreeable. The upshot was that the police were called and Leroy Henry – *sans* knife – was arrested nearby. After being handed over to the US military authorities, he supposedly confessed. He was found guilty of rape and sentenced to be executed.

Even before the case came to court there was much disquiet over the episode. Henry himself claimed he was under duress when the confession had been given and that he had in fact twice before met the woman. On each occasion, he claimed, they had had sex and he had paid her £1 for the encounter. This time however, when he had gone to the house by prior arrangement, the woman had doubled the price (perhaps with an intuition that Henry and his fellow GIs wouldn't be around for too much longer). Henry had refused to pay and the result was the death penalty now hanging over him.

The woman denied Henry's version of events, but there were many who believed him, or at the very least believed there was more to the case than the facts as presented. Even the prosecuting counsel admitted that he found the woman's behaviour, in walking off with the dark stranger late at night, 'rather odd'. The American colonel who presided over the trial however, had no such compunctions and sentenced Henry to be 'hanged by the neck till dead'.

The colonel's decision caused an immediate public outcry and nearly half of the city's population rushed to sign a petition requesting a reprieve. Letters were written to the newspapers, most about the unease felt at the racism that might lie behind the harsh sentence, and a campaign to overturn this perceived gross miscarriage of justice was launched. General Eisenhower, US commander-in-chief of the Allied forces, became involved and thirteen days after D-Day it was announced that the verdict was now considered unsafe due to lack of evidence. Leroy Henry, grateful no doubt to the people of Bath for taking up his cause, was then sent back to his unit, now fighting somewhere in France.

By now, the people of Bath were no doubt hungry for victory. They had won the reprieve of Leroy Henry and now wanted the liberation of Europe and the defeat of Hitler. It would still take almost a year and many more lives of Bath men, but the light was starting to shine, and the end was beginning to be seen.

CHAPTER 10

Liberation to Celebration
(June 1944 – August 1945)

Bath's local division, the 43rd (Wessex) Infantry, had been part of the GHQ Reserve, but by D-Day it had been chosen to be part of the force liberating Europe. By October 1943 it was based in Folkestone and had, since March 1942, been under the command of Major General Gwilym Ivor Thomas, late of the Royal Artillery. He would remain in charge for the remainder of the war. With its emblem of a yellow wyvern, the division now began intensive training for the role which it would play.

The division, as then formed, contained three infantry brigades: the 129th (South Wessex), the 130th (West Country) and the 214th Infantry. The 129th consisted of the 4th Somerset Light Infantry Regiment along with the 4th & 5th Wiltshire Regiments; the 214th included the 7th Somerset Light Infantry Regiment. In addition, there were three regiments of field artillery as well as various other units. Indeed, it was a complete orchestra of war.

Even before landing in France, there had been fatalities within the division. The training for the forthcoming invasion and liberation of Europe had to be as realistic as possible and perhaps inevitably men died as a result. Thomas Arnold Butcher was 32 and a private in the 5th Battalion of the Dorsetshire Regiment (part of 130th Brigade) when he died on 18 November 1943. He came from Oldfield Park, in Bath, and was married to Phyllis. He is buried in Haycombe Cemetery. Another Bath man who appears to have died during training was Corporal Frederick William Robinson from the city's Odd Down area. He was 25 years old and in the 5th Battalion of the Wiltshire Regiment (part of 129th Brigade). He died on 29 December 1943 and is also buried at Haycombe. He was the son of Fred and Lilian, the latter also being the name of his wife.

Although the D-Day landings were successful in establishing a beachhead in Normandy, which would ultimately lead to victory, the cost to Bath men, both within the 43rd (Wessex) Division and elsewhere, was high. Among the dead was William John Comley, a 31-year-old staff sergeant in the RASC who died on 6 June. He is buried in the cemetery at Banneville-la-Campagne in Calvados. J. Stirk was a 30-year-old gunner in the 205th Heavy Anti-Aircraft Regiment when he died on the same day. His wife was Violet Stirk of Lower Weston and like Private Thomas Butcher and Corporal Frederick Robinson, he was buried at Haycombe Cemetery. A further D-Day casualty was that of Dennis Purnell, a stoker 1st class who died on His Majesty's Landing Craft (Tank) 317. He is commemorated on the Plymouth Naval Memorial.

The following day – 7 June – a local airman died. This was Flight Lieutenant Leslie Roy Aust DFC DFM of No.224 Squadron RAF. He is remembered on the Runnymede Memorial. John Frederick Starr, a private in the 2nd Oxfordshire and Buckinghamshire Light Infantry, died on Friday, 9 June. He was the son of John and Amy Starr of Bath and is buried in the Hérouvillette New Communal Cemetery in France. He was 22 years old.

The 22 June 1944 was a particularly sad day for the city. At least three local men died, one in each major theatre of war: France, Italy and Burma. George and Ethel Green lost a 24-year-old son, Anthony Frederick, who was a corporal in the 3rd Parachute Squadron of the Royal Engineers. He is buried in the Ranville War Cemetery in France. 33-year-old George Alfred William Simpkins was a lance sergeant in the 3rd Battalion of the Coldstream Guards. He was the son of Charles and Eliza and is buried in the Bolsena War Cemetery in Italy. 99th Field Regiment RA was part of the 2nd (British) Division fighting in the Battle of Imphal on the Burma front. One of its gunners, 23-year-old Anthony John Watts, was the son of Archibald and Jessie Watts. He is buried in the Imphal War Cemetery.

Along with the Navy and Royal Air Force, there were also Army personnel from Bath who performed acts of heroism that warranted medals, awards and honours. These included Military Medal (MM) recipient James Fairchild, and Philip Comm, who was awarded the Distinguished Conduct Medal (DCM). The heroic act that resulted in Fairchild, of 17 Croft Road, being awarded the MM was recounted in the 15 February 1941 edition of The *Bath Chronicle*:

> Lance Corporal Fairchild, who is a former employee of the Bath Tramway Co. Ltd, was in charge of a Bren gun on a lorry in the Dunkirk evacuation. Suddenly three German dive-bombers appeared and proceeded to drop their deadly cargo in the vicinity of the lorry. Remaining at his post alone, Fairchild opened fire on the three planes who directed their attention on him.
>
> After his first burst of fire the three planes disappeared and later two returned, one securing a direct hit on the lorry, just after Fairchild had got off.

This was only just the beginning of his 'adventures', according to the *Bath Chronicle*, as Lance Corporal Fairchild had to 'face intense bombing' as the steamer he was evacuated on made its way back to England. After this ship became waterlogged, Fairchild spent some time in the sea, before being rescued by a submarine.

Meanwhile, at the other end of the war, Corporal Philip Comm was fighting his way back across Europe, when he was caught up in a 'desperate battle' at the village of Vehlingen, in north Germany. Comm was a platoon commander with the 7th Battalion, Somerset Light Infantry, who at the time was part of the 43rd Wessex Division. Again, the report of a Bath man's bravery was reported in the local newspaper.

A fortnight or so ago we announced that the Distinguished Conduct Medal had been awarded to Corporal Philip Anthony Comm, the Somerset Light Infantry, of Bath, for service in North West Europe. The citation now published shows that this distinction has come to him for courage and resource which had the effect of turning an entire enemy defence line. The citation states:

On 27th March 1945 Cpl Comm commanded the leading section of a forward platoon in an attack on the Autobahn at Vehlingen. The advance was stopped short of the objective by heavy machine gun fire from several well dug-in and mutually supported posts and Cpl Comm's section suffered casualties.

He at once brought accurate fire to bear on the enemy; himself got the wounded back, continued to neutralise the opposition, and indicated the positions to the supporting tanks. Under the tanks' fire this NCO then led his section forward under a hail of criss-crossing enemy bullets. He then, by bold and clever use of ground, crawled right up to the enemy defences and got to close quarters. Thirty Boche gave themselves up; several were dead.

Through brave and skilful advance under exceptionally heavy fire at once enabled flanking platoons to advance and close with the enemy. Cpl Comm's gallantry, initiative and leadership without a doubt turned the whole enemy defence line consisting of an ideal position and trenches full of ammunition.

The 43rd (Wessex) Division, which Corporal Comm served under, was part of VIII Corps. VIII Corps had been established in the summer of 1940 to control the fighting in the West Country had the Germans managed to land there. By 1944, however, it was part of the follow-up to D-Day and once in France, became part of the Second Army. It contained three Divisions: 11th (Armoured) Division, 15th (Scottish) Division and 43rd (Wessex) Division. The latter, as mentioned previously, included 129th Infantry Brigade, based in Bath, and now commanded by Brigadier

G.H.L. Mole. It had three battalions, one of which was the 4th Battalion, Somerset Light Infantry, also based in Bath.

The 43rd (Wessex) Division's baptism of fire was the Battle of Caen. Caen and its immediate vicinity was an important operational objective for both sides – Allied and German – and so it is not surprising the fighting was intense and sustained. On 10 July 1944, the 43rd took part in Operation Jupiter; among the objectives were the capture of villages Baron-sur-Odon and Fontaine-Étoupefour, and to recapture Hill 112 which had been earlier held by the Allies who had been ordered to withdraw after German reinforcements arrived. It had been said by the Germans, 'He who holds Hill 112 holds Normandy.' During the fighting, 4th Somersets suffered horrendous casualties, with 556 killed or wounded out of a strength of 845. Among the dead were Bath men Corporal Herbert Archibald West, 24-year-old Lance Corporal Ronald Payne from Larkhall, Sergeant Sydney Ashman from Southdown and 31-year-old Private Emmanuel William Holmes. Although Hill 112 was briefly captured, once more German reinforcements forced the men off the top. However, despite the failure to permanently secure the hill, the action was a strategic success, as through their counter-attack the German II SS Panzer Corps had been reduced to a state from which it never recovered.

Another unit involved in the Battle of Caen was 5th Dorsetshire Regiment. One of their men, 30-year-old Private James Farnham of East Twerton, died on 10 July 1944, and George Henry Ward, a 21-year-old private in another Dorsetshire Regiment, was killed two days later.

The Somersets – both its 4th Battalion, as part of 43rd (Wessex) Division, and its 2nd Battalion, fighting in Italy – continued to lose men from Bath throughout August. These included Albert Rouen Slip, a 28-year-old corporal in the 2nd, who died on the 5th of August and is buried in the Florence War Cemetery in Italy. He was the son of Albert and Amy Slip and husband of Maud; all of whom lived in the Larkhall area of the city. The following day, two more local men were killed, both from

A memorial to the 43rd (Wessex) Division.

the 4th: Sergeant Eric Walters Lavington, 28, from Bathford, and 36-year-old Private John William Cook. They are both buried in the Banneville War Cemetery in France.

The 43rd (Wessex) Division became the first British formation to cross the Seine river and then took part in the disastrous Operation Market Garden, in September 1944, after being transferred to XXX Corps. The main objective – to cross the Rhine into Germany – comprised two subsidiary operations: the seizure of several bridges by airborne assault (Market) and a ground attack (Garden). Although, like Hill 112, there were early successes in the initial part of the 'Market' element of the operation, failure to take certain key bridges and delay in securing others, including at Arnhem, held up the ground forces (Garden) from successfully completing their own objectives, allowing the Germans to counter-attack and overrun the recently captured areas. The ensuing result was that the Allies failed to achieve their overall objective and would not advance into Germany, as it turned out, until the following spring; dashing expectations the war could be won by year's end. The 43rd continued to have a substantial role in the north-western European campaign – although played a comparatively minor one in the Battle of the Bulge, the largest battle on the Western Front in the war – and by the time victory was achieved had reached the Cuxhaven peninsula of northern Germany, having finally crossed the Rhine river, as part of Operation Plunder, in March 1945.

Like many of the other divisions that fought across Europe from Normandy, the 43rd Division – known by the Germans as the Yellow Devils or the British SS Division – suffered heavy casualties throughout the campaign; most of these being from the infantry battalions, including the Somersets. The overall division casualties stood at more than 12,500 men – 3,000 of these being killed in action – and in many units, this equated to around 80 per cent of their total strength.

Although men from Bath would continue dying in all the theatres of the war until final victory was achieved by the Allied forces in August 1945, with the sounding of what would be the last air-raid siren the city's war was effectively over. The date was 23 June 1944. The local population did not know this at the time and, of course, to all intents and purposes it had been over since the last bomb fell on that fateful Monday morning back in April 1942. The menace had continued to be there, sitting like a dark spectre over the city's skyline, but now, with the Allies making continued headway through France, during the months after D-Day, any further threat of attack was perceived to receding. And since those air raids two years previously, the City of Bath had been tidying up and rebuilding itself. Progress was steady, but by the end of the month (June 1944), John Owens, the city's chief engineer, was able to report that £1,306,495 of repairs were underway. This included the historic Abbey Church House in Westgate Buildings.

On 3 December, the 5th and 6th Battalions of the Somerset Home Guard held their stand-down parades. The 5th (Bath City) showed 1,765 officers and men, plus 143 women auxiliaries, while the 6th (Admiralty) had 960 officers and men, and 77 women auxiliaries.

Each winter of the war seemed to be colder than the one before, and mostly this was true. The Christmas period of 1944, however, was officially one of the coldest on record. Although not actually a white Christmas in the city, nevertheless a 'lacework of ice had spread over trees and covered telegraph and aerial wires with needles of dazzling frost, and produced as white a Christmas as had there been a snowstorm.' Traditional dances 'saw in' 1945 and despite the Germans' last desperate attempt to turn the tide of the war back in their favour, most people believed this would be the last wartime New Year's Day and an Allied victory would be secured sometime in the next twelve months. The sub-zero temperatures remained throughout January to the point where it was being compared to the notorious winter of 1892, which elderly residents of Bath could remember vividly. The Kennet & Avon canal froze solid and became the new, temporary, playground for young skaters.

In the same month as the 43rd (Wessex) Division crossed the Rhine – March 1945 – a Bomb Disposal Squad arrived at the top of the present-day golf course in Victoria Park to recover two unexploded German bombs that had been there for nearly three years. As one of them explained though, they could not come any earlier, as there were other, more important things to be done!

As 1945 gathered momentum, Bath seemed to be gearing up for the return to 'normality', or at least as close to pre-war existence as one could get. The preliminary heat of the South-West Team Dancers Trophy Ball was held at the Pavilion on Tuesday, 10 April; on the 23rd the blackout came to an end and street lights switched back on throughout the city; on 2 May the Civil Defence Service stood down, and eight days later, the Royal Observer Corps also stood down from war duties.

Meanwhile in Europe, Valentine's Day saw the bombing of Dresden, when 2,600 tons of incendiaries and high explosives were dropped on the East German city by 800 RAF and 400 USAAF bombers – killing 50,000 of its inhabitants in the process – and at the end of April, Hitler died. Victory in Europe now seemed imminent and a week later, on 7 May 1945, Hitler's successor Admiral Doenitz offered unconditional surrender.

Celebrations began almost as soon as the *Bath Chronicle* hit the streets with the news, at 3pm as normal, and copies sold like wildfire. Flags appeared in the

'Read all about it' – the Victory in Europe is announced.

Civil Defence stand-down parade, in front of the Mayor.

streets and parties began which carried on until late into the night – festivities at Weston village for instance, which occurred in front of the Crown and Anchor, did not end until one o'clock in the morning, while in Lower Swainswick, an illuminated V was hoisted onto the roof of a house. The following day, the *Bath Chronicle* reported, 'With bonfires blazing in streets where uglier fires had crackled and glowed three years ago, with song and joyfulness and with hearts uplifted in solemn thanksgiving, Bath celebrated VE Day. From morn till night great crowds were everywhere.' In subsequent days, Bath Abbey held a service of thanksgiving, a victory parade took place and the Civil Defence stand-down parade was held on 10 June, followed by another service at the abbey.

In July 1945, 3 FIS(A) disbanded and its aircraft and staff were absorbed by 7 FIS(A). The airfield at North Stoke continued to be used for training purposes by this new unit, but it was only brief, and the RAF handed it back on 22 August. Race meetings started again at Bath (Lansdown) racecourse the following year and soon became part of the post-war racing scene. The site's connection with aviation remains, as these days it has a helipad for use during meetings.

In the same month as the airfield was relinquished by the RAF, spontaneous celebrations broke out once more, as the announcement of Japan's surrender became known. 'Huge crowds thronged Bath streets from shortly after midnight when the VJ news "broke",' reported the *Bath Chronicle* the day after, '[and] until the early hours of this morning, [there was] singing, dancing and celebrating.' Victory had, of course, been secured through the dropping of atomic bombs by the Americans.

With the war now over, thoughts in the city turned to more practical matters. Patrick Abercrombie's Plan for Bath, although creating excitement and hope when unveiled in 1946, ultimately only saw a few of his proposals implemented, and the city remained scarred from its encounter with the Luftwaffe for many years after the war.

Also scarred, both physically and psychologically, were many of the city's service men and women who had fought in the many theatres of the war, traumatised by what they had experienced or else permanently disabled from injuries incurred in battle. On top of this, it took many months for the large numbers of personnel to be demobilised and return to their home city. Quite a few of them had been prisoners of war. One of these was Mr Collier, who lived at 10 Bailbrook Grove in Lower Swainswick; he had been held by the Japanese, who were, of course, notorious for the cruel treatment of their prisoners. Although he returned home, he died soon after.

The authors' grandfather, Ernest Joseph Charles Lassman, came back from serving in the RAF to his pre-war position of chauffeur. When his employer died a couple of years later, Ernest was bequeathed a large sum of money, which enabled him to fulfil a long-held dream of owning his own motor garage business (this was Swainswick Garage, on the A46, which he ran for ten years between 1950 and 1960). Ernest's two sons, Gordon and Ronald (the authors' father and uncle), worked at the garage too. Ronald had also served in the RAF during the war, spending time in Italy, while Gordon, although too young to fight, would follow in the family tradition after the war and spend his two years national service in the RAF.

Like many of its population, the City of Bath would never be the same. In some ways it would be worse, in other ways better. The continuing presence of the Admiralty would offer plentiful job opportunities for the next half century or so, until most of the departments moved to Abbey Wood in north Bristol and the former sites sold off to property developers. Despite the limited implementation of Abercrombie's plan, the numerous bomb sites that existed throughout the city still offered the chance for redevelopment on a grand scale – although many of these new buildings would be sadly out of keeping with the city's Georgian heritage. This would reach its nadir with the 'Sack of

The authors' grandfather, Ernest Lassman, in uniform.

Bath', when the deliberate demolition of many old areas of the city, many of great historical importance, took place in the late 1960s and early 1970s, before public outrage put a stop to it. It has been said that this wanton destruction inflicted more damage upon the city's architectural legacy than the Luftwaffe. Nevertheless, the entire city was designated a World Heritage Site in 1987.

Swainswick Garage, which the authors' grandfather, father and uncle would run after the war.

The visible remains of those two terrible nights in April 1942. A bomb exploded near the Labour Exchange building causing the damage that can still be seen.

There were still many families homeless in the city a year after the war, or at least in temporary (and in many cases unsuitable) accommodation, having seen their homes and possessions destroyed during the blitz. In October 1946 however, some of the displaced families took matters into their own hands and moved into the now abandoned Nissen huts at Charmy Down. By the end of the year there were some forty families there. A year later another ninety families had joined them, and the site had its own school, shop, clinic and church. Shortly afterwards though, new housing was completed for them and they moved away. Most of the buildings on the airfield were then demolished.

Rationing remained and so the post-war prosperity hoped for by many would have to be put on hold for the time being. At the end of it all, Bath had played its part in the national war effort, was perhaps let down most tragically in its moment of need, but nevertheless got up, dusted itself down and continued even more determined to defeat the enemy.

As the following decades unfolded and the city carried on with its future, little was done to remember these years, especially those who lost their lives during the Bath Blitz. But this is slowly changing and now memorials, plaques, gardens of remembrance, books, articles, websites and other relevant projects, including the Bath Blitz Memorial Project seem set to ensure that many more are learning just exactly what it was that these people experienced.

Above: Plaque to the victims of the Bath Blitz, situated on the former Labour Exchange building in the centre of the city.

Right: A commemorative tablet at Haycombe Cemetery, Bath.

Another reminder of the war, though not as welcome, is the discovery from time to time of unexploded bombs in and around the city, one of the most recent being the 500lb one found in 2016 on the site of the Royal High School, Lansdown. A 300-metre exclusion zone was set up and more than a thousand residents were evacuated from their homes after contractors unearthed the wartime device. An Explosive Ordnance Disposal (EOD) team was called to the site and, after the bomb was deactivated, it was carried away on an open-backed trailer by police escort to be safely destroyed.

For those people of Bath who lived through it, the war could never be forgotten. For the rest of their lives, whether they had been in the theatres of war or on the home front, they would carry with them the memories of those years; the sights, the sounds, the smells, and emotions. But, however memories of that period of the city's history surface, whether experienced first-hand or else through other means, it is hoped this book will serve as a permanent record of the time, 1939 to 1945, when Bath was at war.

Left: The plaque commemorating those killed during the Bath Blitz.

Below: The unexploded bomb discovered in 2016.

Selected Bibliography

Arthur, M. *Symbol of Courage* (London, Pan Macmillan, 2005)

Berryman, D. *Gloucestershire Airfields in the Second World War* (Newbury, Countryside Books, 2005)

Somerset Airfields in the Second World War (Newbury, Countryside Books, 2006)

Wiltshire Airfields in the Second World War (Newbury, Countryside Books, 2002)

Brown, D. *Somerset v Hitler* (Newbury, Countryside Books, 1999)

Brown, M. *Evacuees* (Stroud, Sutton Publishing, 2000)

Clarke, K. *The Royal United Hospital* (Bath, Mushroom Publishing, 2001)

Coath-Wilson, C. *A History of the Mayors of Bath* (Bath, Charter Trustees of the City of Bath, 2006)

Coughlan, K, Gale, C and Hall, P. *Before the Lemons* (Stroud, Tempus Publishing, 2003)

Davis, G. *Bath Exposed* (Bath, the Sulis Press, 2007)

Dike, J. *Bristol Blitz Diary* (Bristol, Redcliffe Press, 1982)

Emden, R van. *The Last Fighting Tommy* (London, Bloomsbury Publishing, 2009)

Falconer, D. and J. *Bath at War* (Stroud, Sutton Publishing, 1999)

Bath at War, the Home Front (Stroud, Sutton Publishing, 2001)

Gardner, E. *A Somerset Airman* (Steyning, Red'n'Ritten, 2005)

Gardner, J. *Wartime Britain 1939 – 1945* (London, Headline Book Publishing, 2004)

Hardick, T, Light, T and Ludlow, R. *Basement to Beechen Cliff* (Bath, Old Sulians Association, 2010)

Hawkins, Mac *Somerset at War* (Wimborne, Dovecote, 1988)

Hersey, L and Mason, C. *The West Country at War* (Bristol, Broadcast Books, 1995)

Hill, D. *Bath Fire Brigade and Ambulance Service 1891 – 1974* (Bath, Millstream Books, 2003)

Inglis, R. *The Children's War* (London, Collins, 1989)

Longerich, P. *Goebbels* (London, Penguin Random House, 2015)

Lowndes, W. *They came to Bath* (Bristol, Redcliffe Press, 1982)

McCamley, N. *Secret Underground Cities* (Monkton Farleigh, Folly Books, 2014)

Penny, J. *Bristol at War* (Derby, Derby Books Publishing, 2010)

Rothnie, N. *The Bombing of Bath* (Monkton Farleigh, Folly Books, 2010)

Vivian-Neal, A. *Roll of Honour of County of Somerset 1939 – 1945* (Taunton, Somerset County War Memorial Fund, 1949)

Wilson, J. *The Somerset Home Guard* (Bath, Millstream Books, 2004)

All permissions for photographs not in Authors' collection have been sought wherever possible.

Index

Director of Naval Construction
 (DNC), 11
Director of Naval Land Equipment
 (DNLE), 23
Distinguished Conduct Medal (DCM),
 114–15
Distinguished Flying Cross (DFC),
 103–104, 114
Distinguished Flying Medal (DFM), 114
Distinguished Service Medal (DSM),
 98, 100
Distinguished Service Order (DSO), 100
Divisions,
 1st (Cavalry), 59
 2nd (British), 114
 3rd ('Iron'), 24
 4th (Indian), 59
 11th (Armoured), 115
 15th (Scottish), 115
 43rd (Wessex), 113, 115–16, *116*, 117
Doenitz, Admiral, 118
Dolemeads, The, 52, 80
Dornier Do 17, 66
Dornier Do 217, 66
Dorset, 1, 47
Dorsetshire Regiment (5th Battalion),
 113, 116
Dover, 94
Dowding, Gerald, 54
Dresden, 118
Duke of York, HMS, 99
Dunkirk, 24–7, 58, 93–4, 98, *98*,
 102, 114
 Dunkirk Memorial, 25–6
Durnell, Frederick, 61
 Gertrude, 61
 Norman, 60–1

Eacott, George, 13
'Eagle Day', 44
Ealing, 4
Easter, 11, 97

Eclipse, HMS, 107–108
Eden, Anthony, 31
Eden Villas, 45
Education Authority, 63
Edwards, Bill, 45
Edward Street, 34
Eiffel Tower, 103
Eisenhower, General, 112
Eldridge, Hilary, 101, *101–102*
Eleanor Place, 95
Eley, 34
Elles, Hugh, 84
Elliott, Isabel, 60
 Sidney, 60
 William, 60
Elmcroft, 66
Elm Grove Terrace, 72
Emergency Committee, 16, 87–90
Emergency (Powers) Act, 96
Empire Hotel, The, *6*, 34
Engineer in Chief (E-in-C), 11
England, 26, 46, 103, 105, 114
England (International
 Football Team), 58
England (International
 Rugby Team), 58
English Channel, 24, 65, 98
Englishcombe, 39
Englishcombe Lane, 51
Ensleigh, 34, 37
Evans, D., 58
Excelsior Street, 53
Exeter, 62, 65
Exeter, HMS, 19

Fairchild, James, 114–15
Fairey Battle, 29
Fairey Swordfish, 11
Fairfield Arms, 66
Fairfield Park, 25, 66
Falconers (David & Jonathan), 98
Farnham, James, 116